THE

TURKISH EMPIRE.

A. Frey, Del.

T. Sinclair's lith. Phil.

GRAND SULTAN.

ABDEL MEDJID.

THE

TURKISH EMPIRE,

EMBRACING THE

RELIGION, MANNERS, AND CUSTOMS OF THE PEOPLE.

WITH A

MEMOIR OF THE

REIGNING SULTAN AND OMER PACHA.

BY

EDWARD JOY MORRIS,
AUTHOR OF "TRAVELS IN THE EAST," ETC.

Second Edition.

PHILADELPHIA:
LINDSAY AND BLAKISTON.
1855.

STEREOTYPED BY J. FAGAN.

PREFACE.

The affairs of the East, especially if the result of the present struggle should be adverse to Turkey, may have such an important bearing, that any account, however brief, of the history, political and religious condition, manners and customs, and physical resources of a people who, but a few centuries since, shook the world with the terror of their arms, must be interesting; and the more so from the fact that the Turkish empire seems to be in the last stage of existence, and to be rapidly approaching dissolution.

On the 29th of May, 1453, the Ottoman nation, under the command of Mahomet the Second, surnamed the Conqueror, took Constantinople by storm, and supplanted the cross of Christ by the crescent of the Prophet, on the walls of that capital. The capture of Constantinople was the death-blow of the Greek empire, for a long time previous struck with decay; and the Emperor Constantine, in falling in the streets of that city, closed up the tomb of this empire of the world. Strange and remarkable event! Four hundred years later, the Turks are menaced with the same fate that the Greeks experienced at the hands of their ancestors. Their empire, after being sapped in its foundations by internal anarchy, and by a vicious adherence to antiquated abuses, is, like that of Constantine, in danger of falling by its own weakness. An empire which, in the zenith of its power, possessed forty regencies and four great tributary countries; which had extended its conquests over Moldavia and Wallachia, and which in Europe possessed all Greece, Illyria, Macedonia, Thrace and Dacia, and which had also subdued the greatest part of the habitable regions of Asia and Africa.

Certainly the history of a people, once so great, cannot but be one of profound interest, whatever may be the point of view from which it is regarded. The Turkish empire is, in truth, so remarkable for its religious and political constitution, and it has, in its latter days, given so many occasional proofs of fitful energy and strength, that it merits an attentive consideration. We propose to cast a glance at the history and actual condition of this people, for it is only possible, by studying the foundations of the interior of the structure, to comprehend its deep decay and present precarious state. In this investigation, with no other object in view than a proper elucidation of our subject, we shall be guided by the spirit of impartial history, and the unprejudiced feelings of a disinterested observer.

BY THE TRANSLATOR.

The translation of this work was undertaken, with a view of presenting in a concise form, a general yet satisfactory idea of the past and present condition of the Ottoman people and empire. Although the original work has been preserved, the translator, in order to render it more complete, has incorporated with it portions of the celebrated French writings on Turkey and Constantinople, by Messrs. Jouannin, Van Gaver, and Lacroix, intermingled with a considerable amount of original matter, suggested by his own travels in Turkey and the East. The memoirs are in part derived from the last edition of the Leipsic Conversation's Lexicon, 1854.

E. J. M.

CONTENTS.

FIRST PART.

SECOND PART.

THIRD PART.

FOURTH PART.

FIFTH PART.

APPENDIX.

SULTAN ABDUL MEDJID.

The reigning Sultan succeeded his distinguished father, Mahmoud II., as sovereign of the Ottoman empire, July 1, 1839. Taking the reins of government at the age of 16, and reared up to that period within the walls of the Harem, without the advantages of an enlightened education, he entered upon a task, to the requisitions of which he was deplorably inadequate. His immaturity of mind and character were, in some degree, supplied by the large experience, administrative abilities, and liberal views of his Minister of Foreign Affairs, Reschid-Pasha — one of the most able statesmen that has ever figured in the annals of Turkish history.

At the period of his accession, the empire was in imminent danger of dismemberment. His rebellious Satrap, Mehemet Ali, Pasha of Egypt, had just achieved a victory over the Turkish forces at Nezib, which consummated the absolute independence of Syria, Palestine, Egypt, and menaced the loss of Arabia and the Pachalicks on the African coast of the Mediterranean. Exhausted by the prolonged war of Greek independence, and the subsequent hostilities with Russia, which terminated in the disastrous treaty of Adrianople, the Porte was deprived of sufficient resources to meet the emergencies of the crisis. To add to the public calamities, the Captain-Pasha, a fortnight after the investiture of the new sovereign with the imperial insignia, sailed into the harbor of Alexandria with the entire Ottoman fleet, and delivered it into the hands of Mehemet Ali.

A party was now formed at the capital who advocated the dethronement of the young Sultan, a change in the reigning dynasty, and the elevation of Mehemet Ali, with the right of succession in his heirs, to the throne. This faction was composed of the religious orders, the law officers, and the more fanatical sectaries of the Prophet, who had resisted the reforms of Mahmoud II., as destructive to the religion and anti-Christian policy of the empire. Imbued with a contempt for European usages, improvements, and principles, they regarded their introduction as an attempt to subvert the religious and civil polity of Mahomet, and to establish the Christian system on the ruins of the ancient faith of the country. The selection of his ministers by the young Sultan clearly indicated his resolution to pursue the policy of his father. To arrest such a course, fatal, as they believed, to the prosperity and duration of the empire, they induced the Captain-Pasha to surrender the fleet to the Pasha of Egypt, and organised a vast conspiracy against the government throughout the whole Ottoman dominions.

The only hope of the salvation of the kingdom lay in the interposition of the European powers. Their favor could not be gained but by politic concessions to the progressive spirit of the age, an increased tolerance of the religious faith of the Christian subjects of the Porte, and the mitigation of the social and political abuses to which they were exposed. Reaction would isolate the government from the sympathy of the Christian states, and leave it to contend single-handed against domestic treason and external aggression by Russia. In pursuance of the wise counsels of his cabinet, the Sultan resolved on a decisive step, which at once raised him to the front rank of the enlightened rulers of the age.

On the 3d of November, 1839, numerous tents had been erected in the gardens of the imperial palace of Top-Kapou, called Gul-Khanes. A vast crowd began to assemble in this locality as early as eight in the morning, to witness a solemnity which keenly excited the public curiosity. All the ambassadors and ministers of foreign powers, with the Prince de Joinville, repaired thither by invitation, in the state carriages. Strong detachments of troops surrounded the enclosure. The arrival of the Sultan, who ascended the imperial pavilion, was followed by that of the patriarchs of the Greek, Armenian-catholic, and Armenian-schismatic religions, the grand rabbi of the Jews, a deputation of the *sarrafs*, or Christian and Hebrew bankers, and by all the principal members of the corps of ulemas, the kazi-askers, kadis, mollas, &c. Near the Sultan, and on a separate line, were arranged the mufti, and seven generals of the highest rank. When all were seated, Riza Pasha delivered to Reschid Pasha, the minister of Foreign Affairs, a hatti-scheriff of his imperial Highness. The minister then ascended an elevated tribune, and read aloud this important state paper, which announced the opening of a new epoch in Turkish history.

"Every one knows that in the beginning of the Ottoman empire, the glorious precepts of the Koran and the laws of the empire were held as rules always revered, in consequence of which the empire increased in strength and greatness; and all its subjects, without exception, attained the highest degree of welfare and prosperity. Within the last 150 years, a series of events and variety of causes have, from not abiding by the holy code of laws, and the regulations that arose from it, changed the welfare and strength into weakness and poverty. Thus it is that a nation loses all its stability by ceasing to observe its laws. These considerations have constantly presented themselves to our notice, and since the day of our accession to the throne, the public weal, the amelioration of the state of the provinces, and the relief of the people, have never ceased to occupy our thoughts. Bearing in mind the geographical position of the Ottoman empire, the fertility of its soil, the aptitude and intelligence of its population, it is evident that by bringing into operation efficacious means, we may obtain, by the assistance of God, the object we hope to insure, perhaps in the space of a few years. Thus, full of confidence in the Almighty, and relying on the intercession of our Prophet, we deem it necessary to seek, by new institutions, to procure to the states which compose the Ottoman empire, the happiness of a good administration.

"These institutions should have three objects in view: First, to guarantee to our subjects perfect security of life, honor, and property; secondly, the regular levying and assessing of taxes; and thirdly, a regular system for the raising of troops, and fixing the time of their service.

"For, in truth, are not life and honor the most precious of all blessings? What man, however averse his disposition to violent means, can withhold having recourse to them, and thereby injure both the government and his country, when both his life and honor are in jeopardy? If, on the contrary, he enjoys in this respect full security, he will not stray from the paths of loyalty, and all his actions will tend to increase the prosperity of the government and his countrymen. If there be absence of security of property, every one remains callous to the voice of his prince and country. No one cares about the progress of the public good, absorbed as one remains with the insecurity of his own position. If, on the other hand, the citizen looks upon his property as secure, of whatever nature it be, then, full of ardor for his interests, of which for his own contentment he endeavors to enlarge the sphere, thereby to extend that of his enjoyments, he feels every day in his heart the attachment for his prince and for his country grow stronger, as well as his devotedness to their cause. These sentiments in him become the source of the most praiseworthy actions.

"The assessment of regular and fixed taxes is a consideration of vital importance, since the state, having to provide for the defence of its territory, can only raise the means necessary for the maintenance of the army by contributions on the people. Although, thanks be to God, the inhabitants of this country have lately been freed from the curse of monopolies, formerly improperly looked upon as a source of revenue, a fatal practice still remains in force, although it cannot fail to give rise to the most disastrous consequences—it is that of venal corruption, known under the name of Htizam. According to this system of civil and financial practice, a district is abandoned to the arbitrary rule of one individual, but too often notorious for his rapacity, and the most cruel and most insatiable disposition; for, should this farmer of the revenue not be a virtuous man, he will have no other care but that tending to his own advantage.

"It becomes, then, necessary for every member of the Ottoman society to be taxed according to a fixed rate, in proportion to his means and circumstances, and that nothing further should be exacted from him, and that special laws should also fix and limit the expenses of our army and navy.

"Although we have already observed the defence of the country is a most important consideration, it becomes the duty of the inhabitants to supply soldiers to that object: it becomes essential to establish laws to regulate contingents which each district is to supply, according to the urgency of the moment, and to reduce the time of the military service to four or five years, for it is at the same time doing an injustice, and inflicting a mortal blow on agriculture and industry, to take, without regard to the respective populations of each district, from one more, from other fewer men, than they can afford to provide, and it is also reducing the soldiers to despair, and contributing to the depopulation of the country, to retain them all their lives in the service. In short, without the different laws of which the necessity has been shown, there is neither strength, riches, happiness, nor tranquillity for the empire, and it has to expect these blessings as soon as these laws come into operation.

"It is therefore that in future the cause of every individual shall be tried publicly, according to our divine laws, after mature inquiry and examination; and till a regular sentence has been pronounced, no one shall have it in his power, either secretly or publicly, to put an individual to death, either by poison or by any other means.

"It is not permitted to attack the honor of any individual, unless before a court of justice.

"Every individual shall be allowed to be master of his own property, of whatsoever kind, and shall be allowed to dispose of it with full liberty, without any obstacle being offered by any one. For instance, the innocent heirs of a criminal shall not forfeit their right to his property, nor shall the property of a criminal be any longer confiscated.

"These imperial concessions extend to all our subjects, of whatever religion or sect they may be, and these advantages, they shall without exception, enjoy.

"Thus we grant full security to the inhabitants of our empire, of life, honor, and property, as we are bound to do, according to the text of our holy law.

"As to the other subjects, they are subsequently to be regulated after the decision of the enlightened members of our Council of Justice, the members of which will be increased according to necessity, which is to meet on certain days, which we shall appoint. Our ministers and dignitaries of the empire will assemble to establish laws for the security of life and property, and the assessment of taxes, and every member of these assemblies shall be free to express his opinion and to give his advice.

"Laws concerning the regulation of the military service will be debated at the military council, which will hold its meetings at the palace of the seraskier.

"As soon as one law is settled, in order that it may be for ever valid, it shall be presented to us, and we shall honor it with our sanction, and to the head thereof we shall affix our imperial seal."

After the reading of the hatti-scheriff, Reschid Pasha delivered it to the Grand Vizir, who applied it to his lips with religious respect. The Sheik-el-Islam then pronounced a prayer, to which the crowd responded *Amen!* and the thunder of all the cannon of the fortification announced the close of the ceremony. The Sultan repaired to his palace, where he immediately received the pashas of the first rank, and formally enjoined upon them the strictest observation of the organic laws which his government was about to promulgate in pursuance of the imperial decree. These high functionaries then proceeded to the hall in which the mantle of the prophet is kept, and were sworn to an oath of fidelity by the mufti. A translation of the document was forthwith communicated to the ambassadors of the courts of Christendom represented at Constantinople.

The effect of this nobly-inspired document was to propitiate the public feeling of Europe in favor of Abdul Medjid. In consequence of this and other influences, after an armed demonstration of England and Russia against Mehemet Ali at Acre, on the coast of Syria, a treaty was signed with the great powers, July, 1841, by which the fleet was restored to the Sultan, Syria reincorporated with the dominions of the Porte, and Egypt retained as a tributary country, with the right of inheritance to the Pashalic in the family of Mehemet Ali. The system of reform was energetically prosecuted from this date; the navy and army were enlarged and improved in organization, discipline, and equipment. The condition of the Christian populations of Turkey has been greatly ameliorated since 1839; and the governmental toleration conceded to them presents a highly honorable contrast with that adopted by some of the nominally Christian kingdoms of Europe towards professors of other than the established religion.

The schedule of reform traced out in the Khatti-scheriff, would have regenerated the empire, if vigorously enforced. The corruption and ignorance of the public functionaries, and the comparative absolute despotism of the Pashas, in the provinces, have frustrated the generous aims of the Sultan; and his dominions remain in the same condition in which he received them. The sites of most of the ancient Greek cities, once the seats of large populations, are overgrown wastes; no carriage-roads have been laid out, and the internal trade is carried on as in the primitive ages — by caravans. The streets of the capital are insecure after night; and travelling is exceedingly dangerous, in consequence of the laxity in the administration of justice, and the organised bands of assassins and plunderers by which the country is infested. Whatever may be the issue of the pending struggle, no Christian man can look with indifference upon the wild, desolate, and demi-barbarous condition of the fairest countries of the Eastern world, embraced within the Turkish dominions.

Constantinople has, of late years, become a theatre of incessant intrigue between the leading states of Europe, through their envoys at that capital. The Ottoman cabinet is always constructed in a French, Russian, or English sense; and is swayed by the outside influences of the representatives of those powers. Distracted by these selfish and conflicting counsels, the attention of the Divan is almost exclusively directed to external policy, to the neglect of the domestic interests of the empire. To prevent the absorption of Turkey by Russia, the sovereigns of Europe are always ready to assist the Porte by force of arms; but it may be doubted, if any of them are seriously disposed to aid in restoring the decayed vigor of the Ottoman empire, and of raising it to the position of a self-sustaining power. Whatever, also, Russia may lose in war, she is amply compensated for by the superior address of her diplomatists in treaty negotiations, who rarely fail to achieve at the council-board, territorial conquests which her armies could not acquire in the field. Of this, the most striking example is the acquiescence of the allies in the cession of the mouths of the Danube by the Porte to Russia, in the Adrianople treaty, and the limitation of the newly-formed kingdom of Greece to its present narrow bounds. The latter was an equally fatal mistake with the former, as it prevented the consolidation into a powerful nationality of the only people of the east whose natural intelligence, enterprising spirit, and intellectual superiority, capacitate them to succeed the Turks in their European possessions, and to oppose a barrier against aggrandisement.

Abdul Medjid, personally, is possessed of but few striking natural endowments. His character is timid and irresolute; and although humane and liberal in disposition, he is wanting in that energy of will and force of talent necessary to the crisis in which he finds himself placed. By many he has been compared to the mild and vacillating Constantine, under whom the Greek empire was extinguished by its Mussulman assailants. He is now in the 32d year of his age, and the 15th of his reign. His eldest son, Mohammed-Murad, was born September 22, 1840. His protection of the Hungarian refugees, although it alienated from him the good-will of Austria, commanded the admiration and homage of all the free Christian states of the world.

OMAR PASHA.

Omar Pasha, the commanding general of the Turkish forces on the Danube, is a Croat, and was born in 1801, in Vlaski, a village in the district of Ogulin, thirteen miles from Fiume. His father was lieutenant-governor in this district. His family name is Lattas. In his youth, he frequented the normal military school in his native village, where he was distinguished for his elegant penmanship. He next studied in the mathematical school at Thurm, near Carlstadt; and after he had gone through the course of instruction, he entered the regiment of his district as a cadet. He was subsequently employed as secretary of Major Kneczig, the director of the roads; in which capacity, however, he did not distinguish himself.

Hence he went to Zara; but as he found nothing to satisfy his ambition in that place, he proceeded to Turkish Bosnia. There he entered into the service of a merchant as accountant; and subsequently, on his conversion to Mohammedanism, he was employed by the same patron as a private instructor of his sons, and with them was sent to Constantinople. Here he had arrived at the goal of his ambition, and he immediately cultivated the acquaintance of all who could assist him in the realisation of his aims. He associated with all the distinguished military men of the capital, and soon attracted the notice of Khosrew Pasha, who made him his adjutant. By his interference, he was appointed professor of writing in a military school. Subsequently presented with high encomiums to the Sultan, by the Pasha, he was appointed instructor of the heir to the throne, the present Sultan Abdul Medjid, with the rank of Juz-Baschi (captain), in the Turkish army.

A. Frey, Del.

T. Sinclair's lith. Phil.

OMAR PACHA.

Kosrew Pasha, his original patron, was the guardian of one of the richest ladies of Constantinople, the daughter of a Janissary Aga, who had perished in the slaughter of the troops to which he belonged. This lady he gave to Omar Pasha for wife. He was then promoted to Major, and took an active part in the reorganization of the army. At first he served under the Polish general, Chrzanowski, who directed the changes that were being introduced into the military department. In 1840 he made a campaign in Syria, and was promoted to the rank of Brigadier-General. In 1842 he was appointed to the military government of the Lebanon, in place of Emir Kassan, removed for incapacity, from which command he was, however, not long after recalled, in consequence of his excessive cruelty to the Christian population of that region. In 1843, under the command of Redschid Pasha, he took the field in Albania against the rebel Dschukela, whose defeat was, in a great degree, owing to his skilful manœuvres.

He was next sent, in 1846, to Adschara, upon the borders of the Russian Caucasus, to suppress a revolt headed by Hussein Bey. This was, however, effected before his arrival, and he immediately returned to Constantinople. At this period, the Kurd chief, Bedr-Han-Bei, attacked the Nestorian Christians, and rose against the Porte. He was dispatched with a division of the army of Arabistan to extinguish this rebellion, which he accomplished in 1847, by storming and taking the Kurdish strongholds. The remainder of the year he passed as military governor of Aleppo. In 1848, the insurrection on the Danubian principalities occasioned the joint occupation of those countries by Russian and Turkish troops. He was sent thither as commander-in-chief of the latter. Here an opportunity was afforded him of becoming acquainted with the Russian troops and tactics, and also of the country along the borders of the Danube, and with its means of defence. He thoroughly studied the features of this region, which explains the admirable prescience with which he has conducted the late operations on that frontier of the Turkish empire. He also gained the good will of the people; for while the Russians plundered and maltreated them, he maintained perfect order and discipline in his camp, and enforced a rigid respect for the persons and property of the inhabitants.

On one occasion, a band of gipsies was severely punished by the Russian general Luders, for playing the *Marseillaise* and other revolutionary tunes. Omar Pasha, upon hearing of this, ordered his own music bands to learn the same airs, which he took a particular pleasure in having performed whenever the Russians were within hearing. In 1850 he put down the insurrection excited by the Bosnian nobility against the conscription and the Tanzimat. Upon his return from this expedition, he was appointed to the command of 30,000 regular troops sent against Montenegro. The intervention of the Austrians in behalf of the mountaineers, closed the war before any decisive movement on his part, other than a remarkably skilful arrangement of the invading force, so as to envelope the country with an impassable *cordon* of troops.

Upon the commencement of hostilities with Russia, he was placed at the head of the Turkish forces on the Danube, where he has highly distinguished himself by his successes against the Russians. He is remarkable for his talents as a strategist, and for his consummate knowledge of the geographical features of the European seat of war. He is admirably adapted to the command of a Turkish army, and can hold it in check, or inspire it with the wildest enthusiasm at will. He enjoys the confidence of his soldiers, by whom he is beloved for his frankness of disposition, and minute attention to their comforts. When he received the formal declaration of war by the Porte against Russia, he assembled his troops, and, after swearing them on the Koran, thus addressed them:

"The blood of your ancestors has more than once reddened the earth which a powerful enemy would wrest from us. From your fathers you have inherited a patriotic and spotless courage. Remember that you cannot make a step without hearing a voice crying to you from the earth: 'This earth which you tread is our ashes, the ashes of your ancestors; defend them!' Soldiers! let us swear to shed the last drop of our blood to preserve unimpaired the throne and empire of our well-beloved Sultan, Abdul Medjid."

Omar Pasha is a man of superior mind and education; he speaks several languages besides the Turkish, Servian, German, and Italian. He lives in the European style, with but one wife, a German lady.

CHURSCHID PASHA (COUNT RICHARD GUYON), TURKISH COMMANDER-IN-CHIEF OF ASIA MINOR.

The present commander-in-chief of the Turkish forces in Asia Minor, is descended from a French family, which emigrated to England in the 17th century. His father was a vice-admiral in the English service. He was born in Bath, England, in 1812; and very early in life engaged in the war against Don Miguel. In 1832, on a pleasure tour to Trieste, he formed the acquaintance of some Austrian officers, and entered the regiment of the

Grand Duke Joseph as a cadet; after a seven years' service, he was created first-lieutenant, and adjutant of General Splenyi. In 1839, he married the general's daughter, retired from service, and cultivated an estate in the neighborhood of Comorn.

The political events of 1848 drew him from retirement, and he united with the struggle for independence in his adopted country. In the first battle which the Hungarians fought before Schewchat, October 28, 1848, Major Guyon distinguished himself greatly in the storming of the entrenchments. With equal valor he defended, for an entire day, the open town of Tyrnau, with but 1800 men, against an Austrian force of 10,000 men, under General Simunich. For his gallantry in these actions, he was promoted to a colonelcy; and on the 5th of February he took Branyisko by storm, one of the most brilliant victories of the Hungarian war.

He was recalled by Georgey, the traitor, from motives of jealousy, from the main army, and ordered to the command of the fortress of Comorn, into which he found his way by penetrating, with 20 hussars, through the close lines of a besieging Austrian army. When Georgey became Secretary of War, he recalled him from this post, which he had successfully maintained against overwhelming odds, and sent him to the south, where he fought with great success against Jellachich, and drove him back to Titel. On the 29th of July, he joined the main corps of Dembinski, and participated in the battles of Szovey and Temesvar. After the disastrous result of the latter, and the base treachery of Georgey, he, with General Bem, was almost the only commanding officer who insisted on a continuation of the war. He fled to Turkey with Kossuth, where his military reputation secured him a welcome reception. He was one of the officers whom Austria, supported by Russia, insisted upon being delivered up to them. Abdul Medjid would not consent to surrender him to the vengeance of his enemies; and he was soon after appointed to a command in the Turkish army, and honored with the title of Churschid Pasha. He was not required to change his religion, and yet remains a Christian. In 1850, he was the commanding general in Damascus and Aleppo, in the latter of which cities he suppressed a rebellion, excited by the fanatical portion of the Turks in Syria. He has recently been sent to the field of war in Asia, to arrest the tide of defeat, and restore the order and discipline of the army in that quarter. He is a man of high probity of character, as well as great military talent, and possesses the warmest regards of his troops.

THE CABINET.

I. MEHEMED ALI PASHA, GRAND VIZIR, AND BROTHER-IN-LAW OF THE SULTAN.

MEHEMED ALI first served as sea-cadet on the flag-ship of the Captain Pasha. In 1829, he was introduced into the Seraglio as page of Sultan Mahmoud, and by degrees was promoted to the rank of chamberlain; and after the death of his patron, entered the army as a Pasha. He subsequently occupied several prominent posts, among others, that of Captain Pasha Seraskier. Upon the fall of Ali Pasha, he was made Grand Vizir.

The right-hand man of Mehemed Ali, is Ripik Bey, who unites an unshaken integrity with great talents. Ripik Bey is a warm friend of the English; and they extol him as a radical reformer, philanthropist, and friend of religious toleration, in the broadest acceptation of the term. Mehemed Ali is a discreet friend of reform, and is of energetic business habits.

II. MUSTAPHA PASHA, PRESIDENT OF THE COUNCIL OF MINISTERS.

Mustapha Pasha led an adventurous life in his youth. Born in a small town near Monastir, when eight years old he was carried to Egypt, to see his uncle, Tan Pasha. After the destruction of the Mamelukes, he entered the army of Mehemet Ali, the viceroy of Egypt, and fought in the bloody campaign against the Wahhabites. He acted for some time as governor of Mecca, and in the same capacity was sent to the island of Candia, where he distinguished himself by his humanity, his respect for the rights of all his subjects, Christian and Ottoman, and his efforts to promote the prosperity of the country. He gained the affections of the whole population, who heard with regret of his recall. He is a man of capacity, and decided administrative talent. He is the father of Veli Pasha, the present Turkish ambassador in Paris.

III. MEHEMED PASHA, SERIASKER.

Mehemed is an example of the fact that eminent services are sufficient of themselves, without patronage, to elevate a man to high posts. After the destruction of the Janissaries, he entered the army, in which he became an instructor. In 1827, the plague broke out among the troops at Therapia; but by his wise precautions in encamping the troops on elevated ground, not allowing more than three to sleep in the same tent, and the complete isolation of the sick, he succeeded in extinguishing it in forty days. For this service he was promoted, and finally attained his present post.

IV. RESCHID PASHA, MINISTER OF FOREIGN AFFAIRS,

Was born in 1802, in Constantinople. His father was administrator of the rich possessions of the mosque of Sultan Bajazet. One of his sisters married Ali Pasha, by whom the young Reschid was made his private secretary. In this capacity he accompanied his patron to the Morea, who was there appointed governor. He also acted in the same employment under the Pasha, when he subsequently commanded against the Greeks in the Morea. Upon the death of his friend he was appointed private secretary by the Grand Vizir, Selim Pasha, and served with him in the campaign against the Russians, in 1829. He also acted as secretary of the Turkish plenipotentiary, Izet Pasha, at the treaty of Adrianople. In reward for his services, he was raised to the dignity of Amedzi, or Great Referendary.

He also participated in the conferences with Mehemet Ali at Konieh, and finally succeeded in negotiating the treaty of Kutahea. He was next sent minister to France, for which he was peculiarly qualified by his knowledge of the language and literature of that country, and afterwards ambassador to London. After two years' diplomatic service in Europe, he was recalled. Driven by civil convulsions and the plots of enemies from his country, he travelled through the principal countries of Europe. At Paris he heard of the death of Mahmoud, and his own appointment as minister of Foreign Affairs under Abdul Medjid. In this sphere he earnestly engaged in the reforms suggested by his travelling experience and observation, and is generally supposed to be the author and originator of the celebrated Hatti-scheriff which opened the new reign. Fearing the influence of such an enlightened reformer in the councils of the Sultan, Russian intrigues finally procured his honorable exile to the embassy to Paris, in which he passed seven years. Since that period he has frequently been in and out of office. He is, unquestionably, the first statesman of the Ottoman empire, thoroughly conversant with European politics, languages, and learning, and ambitious to restore the decayed power of his native country. One of his sons has married a daughter of the Sultan. He is fond of the society of Europeans, by whom he is much esteemed for his mild and genial disposition, and liberal views.

V. MUCHTER BEY, MINISTER OF FINANCE.

In this person we have a kiboar, or Turkish gentleman, in conversation and manners. He served for a long time as paymaster of the army, and was once ambassador to Vienna. He has founded a national bank, and done much to repair the shattered credit of the government. He is extremely industrious in his habits, of incorruptible purity of character, and an excellent officer in every respect.

VI. FETHI ACHMED PASHA, MINISTER OF COMMERCE.

This minister has run the career of a courtier. Reared in the Seraglio, he was a long time page, and afterwards second chamberlain of Sultan Mahmoud. Educated to military science by Khosrew Pasha, he figured for a long time in the army, in which he was appointed master of ordnance. He was ambassador to Vienna; and upon his return was created minister of commerce, and subsequently was placed at the head of the quarantine administration.

Fethi Achmed married a sister of the reigning Sultan; this circumstance, and the fact of his being raised in the Seraglio, sufficiently account for the extraordinary influence he enjoys at the Turkish court.

VII. RAMIK PASHA, MASTER OF THE ORDNANCE.

Ramik Pasha travelled much when a young man, and visited all the principal capitals of Europe, upon a tour of observation and instruction. He speaks French and Italian with great facility. For many years he was governor of the Pashalic of Bagdad, one of the most difficult posts in the kingdom, owing to the lawless and rebellious disposition of the Arabs, and the irritable character of the neighboring Persians. Ramik Pasha is an excellent soldier, and a highly honorable man.

VIII. MAHMOUD, CAPTAIN PASHA, MINISTER OF THE MARINE, AND LORD HIGH ADMIRAL.

Of this minister we have but little knowledge. For a long time he filled high posts in the army, and succeeded the Grand Vizir, Mehemed Ali, in the Admiralty.

ABBAS PASHA, VICEROY OF EGYPT.

The persevering efforts of Mehemed Ali to become the renovator of Islamism, the founder of a great Oriental kingdom, and to extend the supremacy of the Arabic race from the Persian Gulf to the Black Sea, were arrested by the intervention of the Great Powers in 1840. The frustration of his ambitious views weighed heavily on the heart of the Pasha, and he finally became so disordered in intellect, that he was obliged to retire from the government, and entrust it to his son, Ibrahim Pasha. The latter died in 1848, and the Pasha himself in the following year, at the age of 70. Of fifty-one children, but four sons and two daughters survived him, the eldest of the former of whom succeeded to the viceroyalty.

Abbas Pasha was in the expedition against the schismatic Wahhabites, and for some time commanded in Djedda, the sea-port of Mecca. He early evinced a strong antipathy to Europeans, and was distinguished for his Mussulman piety, having, on several occasions, made the pilgrimage to Mecca. Upon one of these sacred journeys, hearing of the death of Ibrahim Pasha, he immediately repaired to Constantinople, where he was invested by the Sultan himself with the insignia of the viceroyalty. He has since frequently manifested aspirations after complete independence of the Porte, and for three years he obstinately refused to acknowledge the hatti-scheriff of Ghal-Khane as the basis of his legislation. He has, however, contributed his contingent of troops and vessels to the Sultan, in the war with Russia.

The Pasha has pursued a similar policy to that of his father, whose regenerating reforms, improved systems of agriculture, manufacturing establishments, and efficient changes in the army and navy, rendered Egypt so formidable to the Sultan, and so prosperous in its domestic relations. Since the loss of Candia and Syria, a large navy has become of less importance, and it has, consequently, been greatly reduced. The disproportionate number of public officers has also been diminished, and the system of monopoly which rendered the Pasha the buyer and seller of the entire production of the country, has been abolished. The burdens of taxation have been considerably lessened, and large amounts of surplus income are now appropriated to the support of military hospitals and institutions of beneficence. The erection of the dam, commenced across the lower Nile under Mehemed Ali, for the purpose of regulating the quantity and flow of water in the river, he has ordered to be discontinued, on account of its interruption of the navigation. The humane interposition of the Christian representatives has also induced him to put an end to the inhuman annual slave-hunts on the frontiers of Abyssinia. He has permitted the construction of a railroad from Alexandria to Grand Cairo, which his father constantly refused; and to a considerable extent has lost the aversion to Europeans which he so strongly manifested in his youth. His chief vice is his avarice, to satisfy which he has caused to be worked all the productive mines in the mountains, so long neglected by his predecessors. By penurious parsimony, he is enabled annually to amass large sums for his own private purposes. Through this passion, he is accessible to all kinds of concessions, and even to many in conflict with the faith and interests of Islamism.

INTRODUCTION.

RISE AND PROGRESS OF ISLAMISM.

WHEN, in the first years of the seventh century, A. D., Mahomet conceived his projects of religious reform, there is every reason to believe that his views did not extend beyond the limits of the ancient Arabia. He desired that the land of the patriarch and prophets should cease to be distracted by the religious animosities of a hundred tribes, Christian, Hebrew, and Pagan; and that his native city should be purged of the impious worship of idols, whose statues polluted the first temple consecrated to the adoration of the true God, by Abraham, the common father of the children of Ishmael, of the Israelites, and of the well-beloved of Allah.

All people have had, and always will have, the patriotic weakness of believing themselves more civilized and enlightened than their neighbors. Everywhere, the injurious epithet of barbarian has been applied to strangers. The most exclusive of all mankind, the Jews, who proclaimed themselves the *chosen people*, have left monuments of this national pride, which, even in their extreme exaggeration, possess something that is noble and grand; if, in addition, the Greeks and Romans indulged in this good opinion of themselves, we ought not to be surprised that the Arabs, in the belief that they also were the people of God, should always have been inspired with the same pride and disdain against strangers. They early exhibited a remarkable similitude of manners, customs, and social organization, with the Hebrews; they, therefore, felt but little repugnance in adopting the severe and controlling legislation of Mahomet, who had framed it, after the ancient law; this conformity with the holy books of Moses enabled the son of Abdullah the more effectually to impress upon the Arabs a firm belief in the mission which he pretended to have received from God.

But few legislators have so sagaciously taken advantage of the natural inclinations of men in masses, or as individuals, as Mahomet. If, like Moses, he did not live to see his plans completed, they were perfectly comprehended by the men who inherited them, and who, from the dawn of Islamism, gave them an immense development. Having nothing more to subjugate in the peninsula, they burst from its limits, already become too restricted for their ardent and fanatical coreligionists; the audacity of the Mussulmans did not recoil before two great enemies whom they unhesitatingly dared to brave, for we see them assailing, at one and the same time, the successor of Constantine, and the last of the Sassanides.

During several centuries of almost unbroken hostility, the Roman empire, and that of the Persians, vainly disputed the possession of some frontier provinces upon the Euphrates and Tigris; the hour approached when this ancient enmity was to be buried in one common abyss, and those provinces were to recognize other rulers, and to submit to another religion.

Twelve years had hardly elapsed since Mahomet, forced to abandon Mecca, had fled to Medina, with a small body of devoted followers, to escape the vengeance of the

Koreikites, when Islamism became so powerful, that it precipitated itself upon Chaldea and Syria. The first yielded to Abou-Beker, and in the year 635 A. D., that caliph received the keys of Damascus. Jerusalem capitulated to Omar in 638. The act which consecrated the submission of the holy city, has since served as a model in all transactions of Mussulman powers with people, who, in becoming their subjects, stipulate for the preservation of their religion by means of a payment of tribute. The heroism and enthusiasm of the first Mussulman armies undoubtedly account for the rapidity of their conquests; but the conduct of Omar to the Patriarch of Jerusalem, faithfully pursued by his successors, appears to us to be one of the most powerful causes of the submission of the Christian populations, among whom schisms and heresies had given birth to so many discords and misfortunes. Mahomet had, indeed, prescribed the propagation of Islamism by the sword; the Koran incessantly proclaims it; but the Arabs alone were obliged to embrace it, or forfeit their lives. The tribes, which the new prophet thus violently called to salvation, and to the worship of the only true God, proud of their origin and the primogeniture of their father Ishmael, would not suffer a single Arab to remain a stranger to the national faith, so thoroughly had the son of Abdullah penetrated his sectaries with the conviction that Islamism was the religion which God himself had prescribed to Adam, when he delivered to him the seal of prophecy, and created him first pontiff of the *true faith* (Imam).

The caliphs, successors of Omar, were enabled, by the example of his generous and politic conduct, to grant similar capitulations to the people who sought them. Fear, ambition, and other passions of the human heart, undoubtedly attracted a great number of proselytes to Islamism. They were not repulsed, as by the Hebrews; they were, on the contrary, cordially and eagerly received. If we may justly reproach the victorious Mussulmans for having constrained the vanquished, by menace and violence, to renounce the faith of their fathers, it was only, for the most part, in the first intoxication of triumph, in the sack of cities, or when a protracted resistance had exasperated the victor and inflamed his fanaticism. The scrupulous fidelity of the caliphs in the observance of their engagements, presented a strong contrast with the perfidious policy of the Greeks of the Western empire, and could not fail of exercising an incalculable influence upon the shepherd races, under the dominion of the Byzantine sovereigns.

It was especially in the two first centuries of the hegira, that the work of propagation obtained unparalleled success. This period, so prolific of grand events, in consolidating Islamism as a religion, and as a temporal power, presents a series of facts and results to which it would be difficult to find a parallel in the annals of the world. One-third of the first century had not yet expired, when the empire of the Persians ceased to exist; the last of the twenty-five Sassanides, the unfortunate Yezdedjvid, had perished, 651 A. D., in the river, which formed the ancient boundary between Iran and Touran. But the Oxus did not, at this time, arrest the conquerors. In 664, they had penetrated to Cabool, and the bloody discussions of the Ommiades and their rivals could not prevent the progress of the Mussulman arms into Transaxane and beyond the Indus.

They had been no less successful in Syria, Egypt, the north of Africa, and even on the shores of Byzantium.

The Arabic historians mention two expeditions in 652 and 659, which were carried to the very walls of Constantinople. That capital was besieged in 668, 672, 717, and the last siege had been preceded by great ravages in Thrace. Since 679, the shores of the Atlantic ocean, facing the Canaries, had received Islamism, which has ever since reigned supreme there, preserving to this day its primitive physiognomy. But, before it penetrated into Spain, thirty years later, Cyprus, Crete, Rhodes, Sicily, Sardinia, Corsica, and the Balearic islands, had been subjected by the lieutenants of the Caliphs of Damascus, who became the omnipotent masters of the Mediterranean.

The rapid conquest of Spain, which the Moors could never entirely consummate, opened a new career to the insatiable avidity and burning zeal of the Mussulmans. They soon penetrated beyond the Pyrenees; the glorious efforts of Charles Martel arrested them in the heart of Gaul, but did not prevent them from desolating, for a considerable period of time, the provinces of Languedoc and Provence, and in maintaining themselves at Narbonne, Carcasonne, and Perpignan, and in the country lying between the Cevennes and the sea.

The Ommiade Caliphs at Damascus and in Spain, the Abbasides at Bagdad and Cairo, and the Fathimites in Mauritania and Africa, frequently beheld the Islamism, which they had introduced into the vast regions that obeyed their spiritual power, compromised and impaired by the rival pretensions to the rights and title of Emirilmoumenin (commander or prince of the true believers). Moreover, after the great Haroun-Rechid, and his two successors, Emin and Mamoun, generals and governors of provinces, metamorphosed themselves into dynastic chiefs, and obtained by voluntary or forced concession, the investiture of provinces which had become almost independent of the authority of the caliphs; in the fourth and fifth centuries of the hegira, their temporal power was seriously damaged. Conquerors of the Turkish and Mongolian races soon arose, whose appearance was accompanied by fearful calamities, during which the remnant of their authority was wrested from the feeble vicars of Mahomet. When, at the end of the eleventh century, Rome, frequently menaced in its own walls by the Saracens, conceived the idea of carrying the war among them, and summoned the Crusaders to the deliverance of the tomb of Christ, the Christian invaders did not find their infidel enemies under the command of genuine Arab chiefs. The generals were Turkish or Kurd princes, such as Kilidj-Arslan, Seldjouleide, and, later, the Sultans Eibonites of Egypt, among whom shone conspicuously the famous Saladin (Silah-uddin); for the whole East was alike agitated at the perils with which Islamism was threatened. The single standard, displayed by the Crusaders, issuing from all parts of Christendom, gave occasion to the Mussulmans for the application of their axiom of religious and political law, which designates the mass of infidels or non-believers as *one nation.*

The adversaries of the Crusaders engaged in this sacred war with an ardor and courage fully equal to that of the paladins of the west. We may here admit an incontestable fact, that some benefits were derived from the violent collisions of these great masses, animated by all that can exalt the human mind, and impel it to the most hazardous enterprises. In compensation for the shedding of so much blood, for private misery, and public disasters, the Crusaders brought back with them to the west the elements of a softer and more advanced civilization than that of their ancestors, and some taste for the arts and literature, which were then cultivated in the Mussulman world by numerous celebrated writers and men of genius. The captivity of St. Louis and his illustrious companions in misfortune, fully indemnified France for the sacrifices she imposed upon herself for the deliverance of her king. He returned from Egypt with new ideas; his institutions proved that he had thoroughly studied those of his conquerors. Independently of the literary productions of that period, all of which were imbued with the spirit of the Orientals, whose elegant calligraphy served as a model for the finest manuscripts of the middle ages, the order of architecture, improperly styled Gothic, and adopted in the monuments of the 12th, 13th, 14th, and 15th centuries, was nothing else than the Saracenic architecture, somewhat more ornate, lighter, and elaborated with greater elegance.

Meanwhile, the anarchy which followed the massacre of the last of the Ommiades of Spain, and the parcelling of the Moorish empire into twenty rival principalities, always in collision with each other, and the old Christians, favored the enterprises of the descendants of Pelagus: and when the zeal for crusades to the Holy Land was appeased among the people of France, England, and Germany, exhausted by these transmarine expeditions, the combats between the two religions yet continued in Spain with unabated fury and obstinacy.

This introduction has conducted us to the middle of the thirteenth century of our era; here we pause, for the star of the race of Osman was already breaking upon the horizon.

Thus, by a sort of recompense, when the destinies of the Moors of Andalusia and Granada were accomplished, and they were cast back again across the Straits of Gibraltar into Africa, their primitive country, the founder of the dynasty, called to replace and overturn the Roman-Greek empire, was preparing a terrible vindication of his Spanish coreligionists; Islamism, endowed with new vigor, takes its revenge in crossing, under the victorious sign of the crescent, the strait which separates Asia from Europe; we shall soon see it invade the richest countries of Europe, and for two centuries, menace the rest of Christendom with the yoke, from which Charles Martel vainly imagined he had delivered it.

THE TURKISH EMPIRE.

FIRST PART.

HISTORY OF THE TURKISH EMPIRE TO THE CONQUEST OF CONSTANTINOPLE, IN 1453.

I. ORIGIN OF THE TURKS.

ALTHOUGH the Turkish people — of which the present reigning branch is Ottoman — constitutes one of the most ancient races of the world, it is customary to carry the origin of the Turkish empire, in its more modern signification, only as far back as the conquest of Constantinople. The capture of this European capital, in truth, completed the conquest of the Turks, and founded the Ottoman empire in Europe. Tradition assigns a contemporary of Abraham as the head of the great Turkish family; there is no mention, however, made of the Turks, in history, until after the coming of Christ. Turkestan, a fertile region of Asia, denominated also Tartary, appears to have been the original country of the Turks; hence, they commenced gradually to spread over the rest of the world. They were originally idolaters; and it was only some centuries after Mahomet, and in 960, A. D., that

Salur, then chief of the Turks, adopted Islamism, with several thousand families, and called his people Turcoman, to distinguish them from those who had not yet embraced the faith. Some time afterwards, when the Turcomans emigrated, part to Armenia, and part to the western shore of the Caspian Sea, the first were entitled eastern Turcomans, and the latter western Turcomans; and their new country took the name which it bears at the present day. The Turcomans very early displayed an excessively warlike spirit, and a great passion for territorial conquests. They soon extended the limits of their empire to Sina, and dispossessed the feeble government of Persia of several provinces; in the fourteenth century, their power had already been considerably extended. By degrees, the Byzantine or Greek states along the coasts of Asia Minor, and upon the confines of Europe, were subverted by the invading hosts of Islamism, and converted into Turkish provinces.

II. FOUNDATION OF THE TURKISH EMPIRE — OSMAN.

The Ottoman empire, properly so called, was founded at the commencement of the XIIIth century by Osman, whose history is connected with that of his grandfather, and the emigration of his race from the east to the west.

This scha, or Prince Soliman, at the head of his tribe, numbering about 50,000 souls, emigrated to Armenia about the year 1224. After his death, the hordes which had followed him divided; but the greater part remained under the authority of Ertoghrul, the youngest son of Soliman, and whose son Osman was to appear in history as the real founder of the empire that bears his name.

It was Osman, in effect, who laid the first foundations of a political and religious state in Turkey; and who, by his conquests, extended the bounds of his hardly nascent, and yet limited empire, to the shores of the Black Sea. Such were the beginnings of the Ottoman empire, in 1299. One hundred and fifty years elapsed before it was securely established by the taking of Constantinople, and a century more before it attained the meridian of its glory and power by the conquest of Cyprus, at which it rested for a century and a half. The peace of Carlowitz, in 1698, that is to say, four hundred years after its foundation, was the first sign of its decline; and since that period, it has continued rapidly to decay.

Osman himself already commenced the dismemberment of the Greek empire, in possessing himself of several of the cities and fortified places of Asia Minor; he created also a sort of maritime power, by means of which he committed numerous acts of piracy. In 1307, he made an attempt upon the rich and flourishing island of Chios, with thirty ships, whose crews overspread the country, and massacred the greater part of the inhabitants. A similar fate was inflicted by turns on Rhodes, Samos, Lemnos, Malta, and other islands of the Archipelago. Upon the continent, the same acts were committed; the towns were pillaged and burned, and the inhabitants put to death. While Osman pushed the limits of his empire far into the north, his frontiers to the south were menaced with an invasion of Tartars. Orkhan, the son of Osman, victoriously repulsed the invaders, and obtained possession of the ancient capital of Bithynia, the celebrated Brusa. After this achievement, which served as a resting-place, and which gave a throne to his descendants, Osman died in 1326.

III. ORKHAN — INTERIOR ORGANIZATION — THE JANISSARIES.

Orkhan, the son and successor of Osman, fixed his residence at Brusa, admirably situated at the extremity of one of the most extensive and fertile plains of Asia, on the lower slopes of Mount Olympus, and but sixty miles to the south of Constantinople. In the accession of Orkhan, the younger son, the hereditary right of primogeniture to the throne — one of the fundamental laws of the empire — was set aside by the exclusion of Aladdin, the elder son. The devotion of the former to the speculative sciences, and to retirement, was deemed a disqualification for the sovereign of a warlike and ambitious people. The preference for Orkhan was, however, justified by his magnanimity. He generously offered to divide his authority with his brother Aladdin, in whom the love of study had stifled the passion of ambition; but the latter only desired permission to retire to a village on the borders of the Niloufer; and he even refused the half of the herds which Osman had bequeathed to him. "Since you will not accept," said Orkhan to him, "the horses, cattle, and sheep which I offer you, be at least the pastor of my people — be vizir." Touched with the confidence which his brother manifested in him, he agreed to share the burden of public affairs with him. He was created vizir, which, in its Turkish signification, means a bearer of burdens. While Orkhan, inheritor of the martial genius of his father, was incessantly engaged in wars of territorial aggrandisement, the wise Aladdin, who first bore the since famous title of Pasha, energetically devoted himself to the organization of the government.

Before following the Sultan in his rapid triumphs, we will give a sketch of the administration of his brother.

This study of the first attempts to consolidate a young empire is much more curious and instructive than the brilliant victories which have given it a place among the community of nations. For if the conqueror who opens himself a way across opposing people by his sword, has not near him the firm and moderating hand which renders the yoke less oppressive to the vanquished, and attaches them to their new master by bonds of interest and affection, the conquests of war will be extinguished at his death, if not before; and nothing will remain of them but an empty record. Military force may found empires, but wisdom alone can maintain them.

The Mussulman legislation is derived from four sources: the Koran (word of God); the *Sunna* (word of the prophet); the sentences of the four grand *Imams*, the fathers of Islamism; and the laws emanating from the sovereign. These last, originating from the temporal power, or right of the sword, and comprised under the general name of *Ourfi*, that is, accessory legislation, are only the complement or explanation of the three other parts of the political law; the *Kanounaè* (book, or canon law), is the collection of these laws.

Aladdin first devoted his attention to the coinage; he caused to be struck off, for the first time, gold and silver pieces stamped with the cipher of the Sultan, and a verse of the Koran.*

* The Ottoman money do not contain the effigy of the prince, but only his name, or cipher, engraved in beautiful characters, with the year of his accession, and a number indicating the year of the reign in which they are coined. After the taking of Constantinople, Mohammed-el-Fatyh (the Conqueror), added the emphatic titles of *Sultan of the two lands, sovereign of the two seas, and Sultan, son of Sultan.*

The national costume next engaged his consideration. His first thought was of the turban, that distinctive sign of the people of the East. Mahomet attached the greatest importance to the arrangement of his own. It was formed, he said, upon the model of that of the angels, and was distinguished by two ends of muslin, one falling upon his forehead, the other upon his shoulders. A part of the Arabic nation yet preserves this custom.

Simple caps of yellow, red, or black felt were the primitive head-dress of the Ottomans. Caps of white felt (*beurek*), of the shape of a cabbage plant, were confined to the soldiers and functionaries attached to the person of the prince. On *fête* days they surrounded these caps with muslin, folded with the greatest care and taste. White, symbol of felicity, according to the words of the prophet, *White is the happiest of all colors*, was adopted as a presage of the future prosperity of the monarchy. This head-dress has undergone constant changes. Sultan Mahmoud, the father of the reigning sovereign, laid aside this ancient badge of his predecessors, for the high-crowned brimless hat of red fez cloth, with a pendent tassel, and he has been followed in this radical change by Sultan Abdul Medjid. The primitive turban is now chiefly worn by the Turks of the old school, who resist all change, as inimical to the duration and prosperity of the empire, and as in conflict with the example and injunctions of the prophet.

But one of the most important institutions of Aladdin was the formation of a regular military establishment. Ertoghrul and Osman had no permanent army. They were obliged, for every new expedition, to convoke some time in advance, Turcoman horsemen, named *ekindji* (runners), the only troops then in use. To obviate the serious inconvenience of such a vicious organization, Orkhan created at first a body of piadé (footmen), who received a regular pay of an *aktche* (small piece of silver,) per diem — a very high compensation, when considered with respect to the relative value of the precious metals at that epoch, and to the price of articles of subsistence. His infantry force, divided into corps of ten, a hundred, and a thousand men, was always ready for service. But the pretensions and intolerable pride of these undisciplined troops obliged Orkhan to break them up.

By the advice of Aladdin, the Sultan formed a new force, composed entirely of young Christians taken captive in war, and converted by force to Islamism. This body, which afterwards became so formidable to its masters, soon surpassed the hopes of Orkhan. The Jani-Tscheri (new troop), a name which has been transformed into Janissaries by Europeans, under inflexible chiefs, learned to conquer and obey. After the policy generally pursued by the founders of empires, Orkhan sought to give a religious stamp to this military institution. Hadji-Bektach, a venerable cheikh, founder of the order of dervishes Becktachis, blessed the troop, by placing the sleeve of his robe upon the heads of the principal officers. "The soldiery which you have just created," said he to Orkhan, in an inspired tone, "shall be called Jani-Tscheri; it shall be victorious in every combat; its face shall be white,* its arm formidable, its sabre sharp edged, and its arrow piercing."

---

* This singular expression is employed by Mussulmans as a term of flattery and encouragement; on the other hand, black face is an expression of hatred and contempt. Thus a master satisfied with his servant, will say: *Aferin! iuzun ak alsun* (may your face be white); if dissatisfied, he will say: *Iuzun kara alsun* (may your face be black).

In remembrance of this benediction, the Janissaries always wore a piece of felt behind their caps, representing the sleeve of the holy dervish. A higher pay and more abundant rations were allotted to the new troop than to the other corps. The grades of the chiefs and subaltern officers of the Janissaries, were designated by names derived from the kitchen. This circumstance, ridiculous as it seems, nevertheless had a respectable origin. The Sultan, being regarded as the father of the family, and the purveyor of this troop of faithful followers, those who were appointed to provide for their wants, were decorated with culinary titles. Thus the highest officer in rank was called *tchorbadjibáchi* (first distributor of the soup); after him came the *achtchi-bachi* (first cook); and the *sakka bachi* (first water-bearer); and of a natural consequence, the pot (*kazan*,) which was employed for the distribution of the food furnished by the sovereign, was an object of much greater veneration for the Janissaries than national standards to Christian armies. Around the *kazan* the corps assembled when in council. The loss of this precious vessel was the greatest humiliation that could happen to the corps to which it belonged. A sense of honor caused them to esteem such an event as a great misfortune and an indelible disgrace.

The number of Janissaries was limited at first to a thousand. Every year a thousand Christian children were chosen from the prisoners of war, who were forced to embrace the faith of the prophet, and learn the art of war. When the number of prisoners was insufficient, which naturally occurred in time of peace, the deficiency was supplied by a recruitment among the children of the Christians; a method employed even down to the reign of Mahomet IV., from which period the children of the

Janissaries themselves were enlisted; an epoch from which dates the decline of this celebrated force.

After the Janissaries, the elíte of the Ottoman army, the other corps were organized in the following manner. The regularly paid and permanent troops, of which we have spoken, received lands, afterwards converted into fiefs, with the obligation on the part of the possessors of opening roads for the army during expeditions. The irregular infantry served as scouts and pioneers, and, later, as rowers in the galleys. The cavalry received the same organization. The permanent and paid portion formed four squadrons, composed at first of 2400 men, but the number was soon increased; its position was always in the centre of the army, to the right and left of the Sultan, and of the standard of the prophet. Independently of this paid cavalry, known in the West under the name of *Spahis*, another cavalry force was created, upon the plan of the infantry troops to which lands had been allotted. Its members were denominated *Mossellimans*, that is, "exempt from taxes;" it was commanded by officers, of whom those commanding a hundred men were called *Bimbaschi*, and those with a thousand men under their orders, bore the title of *Sandschakbege*, or, "*Prince of the colors.*" The irregular and unpaid cavalry, not possessing lands, were known as *Akmidschi*. This last, as well as the Spahis, soon became the terror of Europe. The Akmidschi, with others, at the first siege of Vienna, pushed their incursions by Linz to Ratisbon, covering Germany with fire and blood.

These different organizations were terminated when the Greek emperor Andronicus took the field against the Turkish conquerors. Orkhan defeated him, in 1330, at

Pebekanon and Philocrene. The fall of Nice (Iznik), the second city of the Greek empire, destroyed the last remaining barrier against the Ottoman power in Asia. Exhausted by the fatigues of a two years' siege, and by the horrors of famine and the plague, the inhabitants of this important place surrendered at mercy. Far from abusing his victory, the generous Orkhan not only spared their lives, but also permitted them to carry away their riches. Touched by this unexpected clemency, the people presented themselves in a body before the conqueror, and followed him in triumphal procession on his entrance into the city. Upon reaching the gate of Jeni-Chehir, the Sultan was arrested by a sad spectacle; a large body of weeping women prostrated themselves at his feet; they were the unfortunate widows of the Greeks who had fallen in defence of their country. Orkhan kindly raised them from the ground, selected husbands for them among the grandees who surrounded him, and resumed his march amid the universal acclamations of the multitude. This generosity and humanity, dictated by a wise policy, gained him all hearts. A great number of the inhabitants of the neighboring towns, attracted by the magnanimity of Orkhan, ranged themselves under his government; and Nice became more populous and flourishing than ever.

Aided by the counsels of the grand vizir Aladdin, Orkhan gave the greatest care to all parts of the administration. The edifice where were held the oecumenical councils of Nice, was converted into a mosque; and the walls were covered with sentences from the Koran, engraved in letters of gold upon an azure ground. Among others, was to be seen the famous symbol of Islamism, "There is no other god but God, and Mahomet is his prophet." The custom of placing inscriptions on the public edifices, began with this reign. Near the imperial mosque, a *medrece*, a species of university for the study of law and theology, was established exclusively for the *ulemas*, or doctors of letters and law. Besides the mosques and schools, Orkhan founded at Nice the first *imaret* (hospital for the poor), an establishment consecrated to the alleviation of human ills. Bread, two plates of meat and warm vegetables, and a small sum of money, were daily distributed there. The inauguration of this imaret was celebrated with the greatest pomp. The Sultan himself lighted the lamps, and distributed food to the poor. This edifying example was imitated by his successors, whose humanity and benevolence towards the indigent classes, cannot be sufficiently commended. Charity is one of the distinctive virtues of Mussulmans; but the princes of the Ottoman house appear to have always desired to serve as a model to their subjects in the exercise of this touching virtue. Osman never ceased to scatter benefits around him. He never encountered a poor person, without relieving him; more than once he deprived himself of his own cloak, to clothe the wretched beggar. Every day, a great number of the miserable were seated at tables prepared for them in his palace.

Muhammed I. fed, every Friday, all who presented themselves; Bajazet II. sent considerable sums to the governors of his provinces to be distributed among the poor, and especially to the distinguished families, prevented by shame from begging. The sovereigns, the grandees, the opulent, besides the immense sums which they daily disburse in the midst of misery, make it a duty to consecrate a portion of their revenues (one tenth) to benevolent institutions. This inexhaustible charity and generous hospitality, which distinguish the Mussulman, and elevate him, in this respect, so far above other people, is based upon the following precepts of the Koran: "Oh, believers, pray and give alms; the good that you do will be recompensed by God, for he sees all your actions. The faithful, who loves God, must also love his neighbor. It is his duty to succor his relatives, the orphan, the widow, the poor, the traveller, the stranger, the captive, and all who apply for charity. Distribute alms by day and night, in secret and in public; you will be rewarded by the Eternal Father," etc.

The benevolence of the Mussulman extends even to the animal creation, which he is prohibited from maltreating; if the owner of a horse or a camel abuse the animal, the police officers resist their cruelty. The dogs, which a precept of corporal purity excludes from the houses, are fed in the open air by the inhabitants of the quarter, of which they are the vigilant and often very annoying guardians, particularly towards strangers. To kill animals, or to keep them even shut up in cages, are inhuman acts in the eyes of this people. They manifest much repugnance for the chase, and they are often seen buying captive birds, to set them at liberty. These sentiments of universal charity reflect the highest honor upon the nation, which daily puts them in practice. If we have gone somewhat into detail on this subject, it is because we desire to correct the false idea which attributes a character of ferocity to the Turks, judging them only by their excesses of cruelty in time of war; but these atrocities are explained by their fanaticism, which then causes them to look upon their enemies as assailants of their religious faith. With this exception, the Mussulman is good by nature and principle.

The Sultan, possessor of the principal cities of Bithynia,

Nicodemia, Nice, and Brusa, as well as of the capital of Mysia (Pergamos), occupied himself, during the twenty years of peace, which followed this last conquest, in consolidating in his states, the order and discipline established by the institutions of Aladdin Pasha. Immense works signalized this pacific period of the reign of Orkhan. Mosques, imarets, medreces, caravanseras, soon rivalled the establishments of Nice. Numerous cells covered the heights of Olympus and the environs of Brusa. Venerated dervishes, whose prayers and co-operation had aided Orkhan in the conquest of that city, established themselves in these retreats; the pious Gueikli-Baba, celebrated by his mystic contemplations, and his passion for forest life; Abdhal-Murad, who, according to tradition, performed prodigies of valor with a wooden sword; Doughli-Baba, who introduced the use of honey and *yagourt*, or clotted milk; such were the principal dervishes whose names have been preserved by the national writers.

In imitation of the sovereign, many persons embellished Brusa and the environs of Olympus with mosques, convents, schools, and mausolea. The umbrageous slopes of this beautiful mountain, and its delicious valleys, were peopled with saints, learned men, and Turkish poets, who repaired thither in quest of sweet inspiration, or for the purpose of pious meditation. Among the most famous we may mention Molla-Cheiky, the first romantic poet of the Ottomans; Waci-Ali, the translator of the fables of Bidpai; Khygali (the visionary), and Beli-Burader (the mad brother); the one, known for his lyric poetry, the other, for his charming and voluptuous verses; the sheik Albestami, and the grand judge Alfenari, authors of theological and juridical treatises. All these distinguished men repose at the foot of the mountain, and not far from Brusa. This famous city, now the residence of Abd-el-kader, contains the tombs of an incredible number of princes, nobles, sacred characters, learned men, poets, musicians, and physicians. It was the capital of the Ottoman empire down to the capture of Constantinople, and is renowned for its hot springs, its delicious fruits, and its production of silk, large quantities of which are supplied for exportation.

IV. INVASION OF EUROPE BY THE TURKS.

As far back as 1263, a colony of ten or twelve thousand Turcomans, under the command of Saltukdedos, made a lodgment on the Black Sea, whence they were soon after expelled. To this first attempt succeeded a second, effected in 1321, by the Turks, who infested the coasts of Macedonia and Thrace with their vessels, burned the harvests, besieged the cities, and for ten months interrupted all intercourse between them. To put an end to these devastations, the emperor was obliged to sacrifice the crown diamonds. The first pacific relations between the Ottomans and Byzantines date from the reign of Orkhan, intermingled with peace and war, hostilities and alliances. The Greek emperors frequently were imprudent enough to invoke the aid of the Turks, for the adjustment of their domestic dissensions, a circumstance which constantly increased the desire of the latter to possess themselves of the Greek empire. The invasions of Europe by the Turks multiplied in a more decisive and dangerous manner from the incessant development of their naval forces. In 1333, the emperor of the Greeks concluded an alliance with Orkhan, upon the express condition that the latter should respect the towns which yet belonged to the empire. The following year, however, in contempt of treaty obligations, a Turkish fleet of sixty sail landed in Europe, and the fields and towns were again laid waste. Already, in the year 1337, a report was circulated that Orkhan was to arrive before Constantinople with a fleet, to seize that capital. The emperor fortunately baffled this undertaking, which was actually attempted, and the Turks were obliged to retire; but, with a blind infatuation, he contintinued to employ them as auxiliary troops in his army. They finally, in 1357, obtained a solid point of occupation in Europe. Orkhan ordered his son Soliman to make a new attempt at invasion, which succeeded, and put him in possession of Gallipoli, the key of Constantinople, on the Hellespont. Afterwards, profiting by an earthquake, which overwhelmed a great number of places in Thrace, Soliman established Turkish colonies there, and rebuilt the ruined towns. From this epoch, new hordes passed over to Europe from Asia, until the Turkish empire had extended its dominions from the borders of the Black Sea to the shores of the Danube. The capture of Gallipoli, which was the signal of the aggrandisement of the Ottoman power in Europe, was announced by proclamation to the other Asiatic princes, rivals of Orkhan, whose ancestors had shared the empire of the Sheldschukes with Osman. Henceforward, all communications giving notice of similar conquests, were ordinary acts, emanating from the Turkish department of state.

Oppressed by extreme grief at the loss of his beloved son Soliman, by a fall from his horse, Orkhan died of a broken heart in the 75th year of his age, and the 35th of his reign. He was one of the most distinguished princes of the house of Osman, and well deserves the eulogiums which the Mussulman writers have so prodigally bestowed upon him, for his clemency, benevolence to the poor, wisdom as a statesman, and ability and success as a soldier.

V. AMURAT I., THE CONQUEROR.

ORKHAN was succeeded by his youngest son Amurat I., who turned his regards to the west, with the intention of extending the circle of European conquests, commenced by his father. Before putting his projects in execution, he was also obliged to direct his attention to Asia. The prince of Caramania took advantage of the death of Orkhan to attack the Ottomans, whose power gave him umbrage, but he was defeated by Amurat. Reassured by this fortunate result, the son of Orkhan commenced hostilities in Europe by the capture of the fortress of Nebetos, in the vicinity of Gallipoli. In 1361, the largest fortified city of the Byzantine empire, Adrianople, was taken by storm; it soon merited, in a political, commercial, and military point of view, the high rank which was assigned to it, as the second residence of the Sultans. Amurat formally communicated by writing, to his Asiatic neighbors, his brilliant victories, and concluded peace with the Greek emperor, after the taking of Philipolis. Subsequently, in consequence of an appeal made by the Pope, the Hungarians, Servians, Bosnians, and Wallachians, united in a crusade against the Turks, who menaced their frontiers. Hadschi-Ilbeki, without waiting for the arrival of the Sultan, assailed the enemy's camp by night (1363), and put them to rout with great loss of life. The field of battle is to this day called Ssirf-Ssindughi, that is to say, *defeat of the Servians.* Amurat, after this, took up his residence, for some time, in Europe, at Demidoka, whence he directed the construction of his palace at Adrianople; immediately upon its completion, he established himself at Adrianople, which remained the first capital of the empire down to the conquest of Constantinople. After an expedition of five years in Europe, Amurat returned to Asia in 1371, and concluded a new treaty of peace with Byzantium.

A second war against the prince of Caramania, produced by his jealousy of the growing power of Amurat, interrupted the peace which the empire had enjoyed for some years. A battle between the two rivals took place in the plains of Iconium, in which Amurat gained a complete victory. This expedition was hardly terminated, when the princes of Bosnia, Servia, and Bulgaria, united to throw off the Ottoman yoke. Amurat again took the field; he marched towards Bulgaria, obtained possession of the frontier fortresses, and forced the prince to surrender with his capital. Lazare, prince of Servia, prepared to defend himself. A bloody battle was fought in the plain of Kassova, and the left wing of the Ottoman army was already giving way, when Bajazet, son of Amurat, suddenly arrived upon the field with an unexpected and decisive reinforcement. "Already floods of purple blood had changed the diamond-hilted blades into hyacinths, and the steel of the lances glittered like rubies; already the number of dissevered heads and turbans rolling in the dust," says an Oriental poet, "had given to the field of battle the aspect of tulips of a thousand colours," when a noble Servian, of the name of Milosch, penetrated to the Sultan, under the pretext of a confidential communication, and stabbed him with a dagger. The victory, nevertheless, remained to Amurat, but he died from the effects of the wound, in 1389.

VI. SULTAN BAJAZET.

Upon the death of Amurat, Bajazet ascended the throne. Jealous of the affection which the army manifested to his heroic younger brother Yakoub, the new Sultan, justifying himself by the preference of Orkhan over his elder brother Aladdin, caused him to be seized and strangled with the bow-string. This kind of death is regarded among Mussulmans as the most honorable, and is especially reserved as a mark of distinction for the noble, decapitation being considered infamous. Hanging or impaling, the most ignominious form of punishment, is only employed upon robbers and common criminals. In order to lessen the horror of this fratricide, Bajazet hypocritically invoked the maxim of the Koran — "revolt is worse than executions," and added that the sovereign, the shadow of God, ought, as the Omnipotent, to sit *alone* upon the throne. This cruel policy has been unscrupulously adopted by the successors of Bajazet; and the murder, or at least the captivity of the brothers of the reigning sovereign, has become the fundamental law of the state. The Ottoman monarchs founded their excuse for these odious measures in the necessity of assuring to their eldest son the succession of the empire, and of delivering it from those sanguinary contests which marked the early years of its existence; and also of preventing the oppressive expense which the maintenance of so many descendants of Osman entailed, in a country where polygamy is tolerated by law. The force of this latter reason can be better illustrated by an example. The Caliph Abdullah III. having ordered, in 1316, the census of the house of the Abassides, found that it numbered *thirty-three thousand* princes, or princesses!

Bajazet filled Servia with Turkish colonies, and then made peace, but upon severe conditions for the vanquished. In 1390, he directed all his forces against Europe, after having strongly fortified Gallipoli, and provided it with a secure harbor. The Byzantine emperor was obliged to furnish auxiliary troops to the Turkish army, and to send his son and successor with them. The Turks first turned their arms against the Archipelago, and took Lemnos, Rhodes, Chios, Eubea, and Attica. The Greek prince having abandoned the Turkish army, Bajazet, in his fury, marched against the Greek empire, laying waste the whole country with fire and sword, up to the walls of Constantinople, where he made the first siege of that city, which lasted for seven years. Wallachia surrendered, and became tributary to the Porte. Another part of the Turkish army invaded Bosnia, and penetrated to the frontiers of Hungary. Availing himself of this distant march, the Prince of Caramania made another effort at insurrection; but he was again beaten, and the Turks improved this victory by pushing their conquests yet farther in Asia.

Intoxicated by his successes, Bajazet surrendered himself to the most unbridled debauchery, and contributed not a little to the development of the already extensive demoralisation. About this epoch [1394], Sigismund, king of Hungary, formed an alliance with several of his allies, to check the incursions of the Turks. France sent a thousand cavaliers, and six thousand mercenaries. This troop was joined, in its passage through Germany, by Frederic, Count of Hohenzollern, at the head of the German nobles; by the Grand Master of the order of St. John, with a considerable number of the knights; and by many Bavarian and other nobles. The allied army concentrated at Nicopolis. The battle commenced the 20th of September, 1396, and terminated in a splendid victory to Bajazet, and the complete defeat of the allies. The banner of Sigismund was overthrown, and all the Bavarian nobles who rallied around it, perished to the last man. King Sigismund and the chiefs of the army took to flight, and with difficulty gained their fleet, aboard of which they took refuge. After the victory, Bajazet established his camp under the walls of Nicopolis. Upon learning that his loss amounted to 50,000 men, he shed tears of rage, and swore to avenge the death of his followers; all the prisoners, to the number of 10,000, were massacred, with few exceptions, by his orders. The carnage lasted from sunrise to four o'clock in the afternoon. At this moment, the nobles of the empire threw themselves at the feet of the Sultan to implore his clemency, and pardon was granted. The principal persons among the prisoners could only be redeemed with immense ransoms. Ten thousand ducats were paid for some. The liberty of the French prisoners cost 200,000 ducats. The Sultan dismissed the Count of Nevers with these words: "I release you from your oath never more to bear arms against me; I advise you, on the contrary, if you have any ambition, to resume them as soon as possible, and to rally around you all the forces of Christendom. You could not do me a greater pleasure than to furnish me an opportunity of acquiring new glory."

From Brusa, whither he had repaired, Bajazet filled all Asia with the fame of his brilliant victory. Ambassadors were charged to communicate it, in form, to the different people of Asia; to give a more impressive character to their mission, the Sultan caused them to be accompanied by sixty nobles, and a Hungarian magnate, selected from among the prisoners, whom he offered as presents to the Oriental monarchs. One of the first consequences of this victory of the Turks, was the taking of Mitrowiz, upon the Save, in 1396; and their invasion of Styria, into which they penetrated as far as Pettau, and reduced it to ashes.

The Sultan now applied all his energies to the reduction of Constantinople, which he had besieged for five years. The inhabitants began to murmur, and to manifest a desire to surrender to the Turks, rather than to suffer any longer the torments of famine. The emperor, at a loss what part to take, resolved to grant to the Sultan at Constantinople, the capital of the Christian world, the privilege of erecting a mosque, and the nomination of a Cadi. This was the fourth mosque which this too complaisant Christian sovereign had allowed the Turks to erect upon his territory. Sultan Bajazet also obtained permission to people one of the faubourgs of the city with Turkish colonists, and to establish a special tribunal for the latter. After having thus humiliated the chief of the Byzantine empire, in his own capital, Bajazet, rapid as the lightning, crossed into Asia, where his general, Timurtatsch, was engaged in extending his frontiers to the north and east, while he himself pushed them to the south and west. Timurtatsch carried his victorious standards to the banks of the Euphrates; and Bajazet invaded Greece, where he occupied the principal towns of Thessaly, almost without resistance, and afterwards conquered the whole of that country, with the peninsula of the Morea.

After so many triumphs, he returned to Brusa, where, surrounded by slaves of both sexes, of a rare beauty, he abandoned himself without fear to the most culpable pleasures. The annunciation of the approach of Timour, the celebrated chief of the Tartars, aroused him from his voluptuous repose. The conqueror of the world, and head of the Tartar tribes, Timour, that is to say, *iron*, had subjugated Persia, and the greater part of Central Asia, when he declared war against Bajazet for insults to his ambassadors. Before Aleppo, Timour met the Egyptian army, which he entirely defeated; he then marched upon Damascus, and carried it by assault; and followed up his successes by the sacking of Bagdad. Bajazet, confident in his hitherto uninterrupted good fortune, proceeded to meet Timour, and attacked him in the plains of Angora. Four sons of the Tartar sovereign, and five sons of the Ottoman monarch, commanded in the armies of their fathers. The combat between the two greatest conquerors of the age began at six o'clock in the morning, and lasted till night. Bajazet performed prodigies of valor. Abandoned by the troops of Aidin, who recognised their prince in the ranks of Timour, and by the auxiliary Tartars, the heroic Sultan, at the head of his ten thousand Janissaries, resisted the attacks of the enemy throughout the entire day. It was only when those brave warriors were crushed by fatigue, or nearly annihilated, that Bajazet resolved to fly. But a fall from his horse having arrested him in his flight, he was taken prisoner, with one of his sons. The unfortunate Bajazet, obliged to follow the Tartar chief in his conquests, was attacked by a profound melancholy, and died in his rigid captivity, March 9th, 1403. This Sultan was one of the most brilliant soldiers in the annals of the Ottoman empire. From the rapidity of his movements, and his promptitude of decision, he was surnamed *the lightning* by the Turks. Reserved and taciturn, he rarely communicated his designs to any one; sagacious in seizing upon the propitious moment, he suddenly appeared in Europe, when he was supposed to be engaged in the heart of Asia; for fourteen years he kept both continents in a state of anxious suspense. Although prone to anger, he was by nature just, and his sudden gusts of passion soon gave way to a calm serenity of mind, and to clemency of conduct. His history is one of the striking illustrations of the caprices of fortune, which from time to time seems to take pleasure in elevating men to the summit of human greatness, that their fall may be more startling and impressive.

THE SULTANS MAHOMET I. AND AMURAT II.

Mahomet the First succeeded his father Bajazet, and ascended the throne, after having previously got rid of his brothers by virtue of the law, to which we have already alluded. One of the first cares of his government, in 1413, was the renewal of the treaties of peace with the monarchs of Christendom, with the exception of the prince of Caramania, upon whom he inflicted a signal chastisement. The following year, he was unsuccessful in a naval action with the Venitian fleet before Gallipoli, and was forced into a disadvantageous peace; an expedition to Hungary also failed, and the tranquillity of the empire was disturbed by domestic insurrections. Mahomet died suddenly in 1421. His death was concealed for forty days, in order to give time to his son and successor, Amurat II., to arrive from Brusa and ascend the throne of his father. Amurat II. continued the siege of Constantinople by Mahomet I. In 1422, ten thousand cavaliers appeared before that city, after having laid waste the country through which they marched. Amurat, himself, soon after presented himself at the head of a large body of infantry, to storm the city, but the ramparts resisted the artillery of the besiegers. A general assault was then undertaken; happily for Constantinople, its whole population flew to arms, and by courageous perseverance, saved it from the furious onset of the Turks, who were repulsed with great loss. In 1428, Amurat made a new treaty of peace with Hungary and Servia, by which the latter country imposed upon itself an annual tribute of 50,000 ducats. This point settled, he marched upon the fortress of Bressatonika, which had been sold to the Venitians, and which was to be returned to the Turks in 1430. The latter took it, after a hard contest, and rushed upon the inhabitants like a pack of carnivorous animals, massacring them without distinction of age, sex, or condition, and devoting the place to a general sack. Amurat subsequently repeopled it with Turkish colonists, and transformed the churches into mosques. In the following years, new expeditions were made into Wallachia and Transylvania. Hermanstadt was besieged, in vain, for eight days; the suburbs of Cronstadt were burned, the whole country ravaged during forty-five days, and 70,000 inhabitants were carried off into slavery.

It was before the celebrated fortress of Belgrade, that Amurat, in 1440, met, in the person of the Hungarian, John Hunyady, a rival of equal prowess and ability. The latter raised the siege of Hermanstadt, and attacked the Turkish army with such success as to slay twenty thousand of its number. At the battle of Vatag, the Hungarians likewise gained a victory, and took two hundred Ottoman standards. The next year, 1443, a new crusade of Hungarians, Poles, Servians, Wallachians, and Germans, took place against the Porte. John Hunyady invaded Servia, advancing as far as Nissa, where he beat the Turks. In a second battle, no less decisive, in the plains of Jalovaz, the Turks were again defeated. Amurat being forced at the same time to maintain a serious struggle with the prince of Caramania, evinced a disposition to accept propositions of peace, which was finally concluded in July, 1444, at Szegedin; Servia was to be restored to its legitimate prince, and Wallachia remained under the Hungarian protection.

After a stormy reign of twenty-three years, Amurat, feeling the necessity of repose from his fatigues, yielded the reins of government to his son; but when, some time afterwards, Wladislas, king of Poland, broke the armistice, he re-assumed power, to march against the enemy, and chastise the perjurers. The two belligerent armies, on the 10th of November, 1444, met before Varna, and a brilliant victory recompensed Amurat for his valor and military skill. The booty was immense. Amurat a second time laid aside power, and remitted the government again to his son. But he did not fail to perceive that the latter, but sixteen years of age, was not yet able to support the burdens of state. He re-ascended the throne, for the third time, and directed his attention to the south of the Byzantine empire, to the Peloponnesus and Albania. In the spring of the succeeding year, the Sultan marched against Albania, but an invasion of John Hunyady, in Servia, soon recalled him to a conflict with the latter, whom he defeated near Kassova, the 18th of October, 1448. The *elíte* of the Hungarian nobility heroically fell fighting on the field of battle, and the contest lasted three days. John Hunyady a second time saved himself by flight, and was replaced by Skanderberg, equally famous as himself. For twenty-five years, this redoubtable chief, whose real name was George Castriota, and his title, Iskander-Bey, that is, Prince Alexander, maintained a bloody struggle against the Mussulmans. His daring exploits, characterised as well by great military talent as by desperate courage, enabled him, on several occasions, to defeat the Turks, and to prevent the subjection of his native Albania. His extraordinary actions partake of the fabulous, and have furnished exhaustless themes of poetic commemoration to Greek eulogists. The Sultan retired to Adrianople, where he was solicited to lend his aid in raising Constantine to the Greek throne, which he did. Not long after, in 1450, he died, and Mahomet II, his son and successor, definitively took possession of the government.

During the thirty years of his reign, Amurat contributed greatly to the power and glory of the empire. His character was just and firm; if, as a true philosopher, he preferred the happiness of private life to the splendor of the throne, he knew when to tear himself from it at the call of his country, and to assume the cares of state. Pious and charitable, as almost all the princes of the dynasty of Osman were, his first care, on obtaining possession of an enemy's town, was to erect a cathedral, a mosque, an imaret, a medrece, and a khan. The mosque of Adrianople, one of the most beautiful structures of the empire, was his work, as well as the vast bridge thrown over the marsh between Salonica and Yeni-Chehir, and that of seventy-one arches at Erkene, and another at Angora. The toll of the latter was dedicated to the relief of the poor of Mecca and Medina, to whom the Sultan annually sent a donation of 3500 ducats at the departure of the pilgrim caravan. The organization of the army was much improved, and particularly the Janissary corps.

VIII. MAHOMET II. SIEGE AND FALL OF CONSTANTINOPLE.

Mahomet II. received congratulatory deputations at Adrianople from all the Christian powers with whom he entertained amicable relations. He renewed all the treaties of peace, and also that with the prince of Caramania, although he then cherished the intention of declaring war against Byzantium. Some months after, he determined upon the construction of a fort upon the European shore of the Bosphorus, directly facing that raised by Bajazet on the opposite shore. He thus proposed to render himself master of the communication between Constantinople and the Black Sea. On hearing of this, Constantine, in great alarm, immediately despatched ambassadors to the Sultan, offering him tribute, and implored him to renounce his project. The Ottoman monarch replied, that no one had the right to object to works which it pleased him to erect on his own territory; that both shores belonged to him; that of Asia, because it was in the possession of the Mussulmans, and that of Europe, because the Christians could not defend it. He terminated with an order to the Greek envoys to retire; at the same time threatening to flay alive whoever should again bring him a similar message. He then set about the construction of the fort. The Sultan himself directed a part of the works, and entrusted the supervision of the remainder to his vizirs. Six thousand masons and mechanics were employed in the building of this formidable fortress. Besides the materials transported from Asia, the ruins of many houses and churches on the Bosphorus were made use of. The fort was finished in three months, and garrisoned by four hundred Janissaries. The commander was ordered to allow the passage of vessels of all nations on the payment of a fixed tribute.

To breach the walls of Constantinople, which promised a long and troublesome resistance, the Sultan caused cannon of fabulous calibre to be founded, one of which is without an equal in the history of artillery. This cannon fired stone balls, nine feet in diameter, the distance of a mile. The report of the discharge could be heard for several leagues; and it required fifty pair of oxen to drag it along, and one hundred men for its transportation and service.

Situated in the most magnificent position at the extremity of the European shore of the Bosphorus, the ancient Byzantium is built, like Rome, upon seven hills. When Constantine, in 330, selected it for the imperial residence, he changed its first name into that of Constantinopolis (city of Constantine). By the Turks, from the perversion of the Greek words εις την πολιν (to the city), it is called Istambol, or Stamboul. Its form is triangular; the base of the triangle rests upon the continent of Europe on the west; it is defended by a double ditch, and a double line of fortifications. The two other sides are bounded to the south by the sea of Marmora, and to the north-east by a harbor, about three and a half miles long, and half a mile broad, which was called the Golden Horn by the Greeks; it is one of the best and most secure ports in the world. A single wall defends this double shore. At the time of the siege of Constantinople by Sultan Mahomet II., a heavy fortress was erected at each point of the triangle.

Alarmed by the immense preparations of the Sultan, and having a presentiment of the fall of their capital, the Greeks at this moment recalled all the sinister predictions which had so long been current among them. Two gates of the city, the *Golden Gate*, and that called *Cercoporta*, had been walled up on account of a prophecy that the conquerors would enter the city by them. This tradition is likewise preserved among the Mussulmans; they in their turn are persuaded that the Christians will some day get possession of Stamboul through the Golden Gate, which gives access to the circuit of the seven towers. As to the Turks, their confidence was fortified by the words of the prophet, assuring them of the acquisition of a new capital for the Mohammedan faith, under the war-cry of "God is great, and Mohammed is his prophet."

On the first Friday after Easter, 6th of April, 1453, Mahomet appeared before Constantinople with an army of 250,000 men, and a fleet of 420 vessels, of all sizes. The number of armed Greeks did not exceed 5000 men, to which may be added 3000 strangers, who had repaired to the defence of the capital. Fourteen vessels, furnished by the allies, formed the entire fleet. Upon the land side fourteen batteries were erected, in one of which was placed the colossal cannon founded at Adrianople. It had required two months to transport it a distance of 108 miles; when it was in motion, it was preceded by 250 pioneers and carts, drawn by an hundred oxen, and sustained in equilibrium by 400 men. Placed before one of the gates of the city, it burst, killing the Hungarian who had founded it. Two hours were necessary to load it, and it could be fired but eight times in the course of a day. A naval action occurred the 15th of April, before Constantinople, which the Turks lost, notwithstanding their numerical superiority. Not finding any means of penetrating with his fleet into the harbor, the entrance of which was closed by a chain, the Sultan conceived the bold idea of transporting his vessels by land. This toilsome but not impossible operation, of which there were several examples in antiquity, was executed with great skill and success. A space of six miles was laid with planks, coated with grease. More than seventy vessels were pushed over this road in a single night; and on the morrow they were seen at anchor in the midst of the harbor of Constantinople, to the infinite surprise and consternation of the Greeks. The Genoese allies of the Turks attempted in vain to burn the fleet. Master of the port, Mahomet established a bridge across it, by means of casks secured to each other by iron cramps, and surmounted by planks firmly fastened together. The besieged in vain endeavored to destroy it by means of the Greek fire; but the vigilance of the Mussulmans foiled these efforts. After fifty days of siege, during which the Ottoman artillery had prostrated four towers, and opened a large breach at the St. Roman gate, the Sultan, through his son-in-law, summoned Constantine to surrender. The emperor nobly replied that he would defend to the last breath the empire which God had intrusted to his care.

Upon the receipt of this answer, the Sultan made every preparation for a general attack by land and sea. He promised to his soldiers all the city as booty, with the exception of the land and the edifices, which he reserved to himself. Loud shouts of joy hailed this promise. Premiums were offered to those who should first mount the ramparts, while the cowardly were menaced with instant death, if they should attempt to fly. The dervishes ran about the camp, promising the protection of the prophet to the soldiers, and constantly repeating the words, "There is no other god but God, and Mahomet is his prophet." At night, a general illumination lighted up the shores of the Bosphorus, and the heights of Galata. Dances and joyous songs celebrated, in advance, the fall of Constantinople; whilst the besieged, terror-struck, and seized with a sombre presentiment, prostrated themselves in tears before the image of the Virgin, whose miraculous interposition had so often delivered them from the assaults of the Ottomans. In this critical hour, the emperor himself visited all the posts, haranguing the troops, and resorting to every means that could stimulate their drooping valor.

On the 29th of May, at daybreak, the besiegers commenced operations. Two hours of desperate and obstinate fighting elapsed before the victory was decided. To the efforts of the Turks, the Greeks opposed the courage of despair; the terrible Greek fire set the vessels in flames; a storm of arrows and stones poured, like hail, upon the assailants. At this decisive moment, the Ottoman troops, on the point of giving way, were rallied by the exhortations of the Sheiks Ahmed Kourani, and Ak-Chems-Uddin, who repeated aloud the extracts from the Koran relative to the taking of Constantinople. Finally, fifty Turks penetrated into the city by the gate of Cercoporta, which, by an inconceivable negligence, had been left open; the Greeks, struck with consternation, precipitated themselves towards the northern shore; the soldiers who guarded it closed the gates, and threw the keys into the sea. The fugitives then fled to the church of St. Sophia, awaiting in vain the coming of the angel, who, according to a prediction circulated among the people, was to repulse the enemy. But the gates of the temple were hewn down by the axe of the victors, and no miracle came to the rescue of the Christians.

Constantine, who was fighting in the breach, seeing the rout of his troops, threw himself among the Turks, and gloriously perished in the midst of his enemies. From this instant, pillage, conflagration, and profanations of all kinds, signalised the triumph of the Turks. When the city was entirely subdued, the Sultan made his triumphal entry by the St. Roman gate ; he halted before the church of St. Sophia, alighted from his horse, and inspected it in detail, with expressions of the liveliest admiration for this superb temple. He was the first to ascend the altar, which he immediately dedicated to Islamism.

The body of Constantine, recognisable by purple boots, bespangled with golden eagles, was found among the dead; his head was at first placed upon a column of porphyry in one of the public squares, and was afterwards carried around for exhibition among the towns of Asia.

When Mahomet arrived at the imperial palace, he was forcibly impressed by the gloomy solitude and emptiness of the apartments, once so brilliant and animated; he recited aloud, at this sad spectacle, a Persian distich, "The spider has woven his web in the palace of the Cæsars; the owl causes the dome of Efrasiab to resound with its nocturnal wail." This philosophic reflection did not prevent the Sultan from abandoning himself to the most extravagant intoxication at his triumph, and to acts of cruelty. The grand duke, Nataras, and his sons, excepting the youngest, reserved for the service of the Sultan, as a page; Spanish and Venitian nobles, and Greek lords, all perished, victims of the ferocity of the conquerors. At last, after the three days of pillage, which he had promised to the army before the assault, the Sultan felt it necessary to put an end to these scenes of devastation. He recalled the Greeks to the city, caused new buildings to be erected, and the mutilated monuments to be repaired. He even conceded to the vanquished the free exercise of their religion, and allowed them all the churches, from that of the Armenians to the gate of Adrianople. Such was the memorable siege of Constantinople, which delivered that city to the Mussulmans the 29th of May, 1453, eleven hundred and twenty-five years after its rebuilding by Constantine the Great, and eight hundred and fifty-seven years after the hegira, or flight of the prophet.

SECOND PART.

HISTORY OF THE TURKISH EMPIRE FROM THE CONQUEST OF CONSTANTINOPLE TO THE PEACE OF CARLOWITZ, 1699.

I. MAHOMET II., THE CONQUEROR.

As soon as Mahomet saw himself absolute master of Constantinople, as a true statesman, he devoted himself to the securing of his conquest by political institutions in harmony with the manners and customs and wants of his new subjects. To gain the affections of the Christians, he respected their faith and their usages, and desired that, in place of the patriarch, who had just died, a new spiritual chief should be chosen, according to the forms that had always been observed. As soon as George Scholarius had been invested with the new dignity, the Sultan gave him a magnificent banquet, during which he conversed in the most friendly and familiar manner with him. He then presented him with a precious sceptre, emblem of the religious and civil authority which he had just confided to him, and thus addressed him: "Be patriarch, and may heaven protect you! In every event, count upon my friendship, and enjoy all the privileges which your ancestors possessed." After these noble words, the Sultan himself reconducted the prelate to the court of the palace, and ordered the viziers and pashas who surrounded him to escort him to his residence.

The following year, Mahomet wrote to the Servian prince, in a few simple terms, that that principality belonged to him, and that he was going to take possession of it. George repaired to Hungary in quest of succor, and Mahomet invaded his states. The people threw themselves into the fortresses, to which the Sultan laid siege, while his cavalry overran the country, and took about 50,000 prisoners, a part of whom were sent to Constantinople, to repeople it. The principal Servian fortress, Ostrowitz, was taken by storm, and its garrison made prisoners. Upon these successes, John Hunyady, who had reassembled an army in Hungary, concluded a new treaty of peace with the Sultan, upon the condition of an annual tribute.

Impatient of new conquests, the Sultan at the same time gave orders to his fleet to go to sea, and secure possession of several of the islands of the Archipelago, the result of which expedition was the incorporation of Lesbos, Lemnos, Chios, and others, with the Turkish empire. In 1456, Mahomet again took the field, and marched against Hungary. He appeared before Belgrade with 300 pieces of artillery, and cannonaded the fortress night and day. The grand lieutenant and governor of the empire, John Hunyady, who had reunited the army of the crusaders, upon the appeal of the Pope, commenced his movements by defeating the Turkish fleet upon the Danube. Mahomet had already obtained possession of the suburbs of Belgrade, when the crusaders fell upon his army with great fury, and obliged him to retire, after suffering severe losses. The next year, the Sultan caused Servia to be ravaged by one of his generals, while he himself undertook the campaign of Greece. The important point of that kingdom, at that time, was the Morea, where two princes, constantly embroiled with each other, yet maintained a show of power. Mahomet availed himself of these domestic dissensions, which distracted the country, to invade it. Athens and the principal towns, one after another, fell into his hands, and in a short time, with the exception of a few fortified sea-coast towns belonging to the Venitians, he had subjugated the whole of Greece.

Mahomet then proceeded to Asia with his army, to continue his conquests. After subduing Sinope, he marched on Trebisond; and that shadow of the ancient Greek empire vanished at his approach. As the Byzantine power had been extinguished in blood and ignominy in the east and the west, so was the Greek empire destroyed in Europe and Asia, by the "master of two seas and of two continents," as Mahomet styled himself after the capture of Constantinople. The Sultan had hardly returned from Trebisond, when he was obliged to resume his arms, in order to chastise the Waiwode of Wallachia, a cruel tyrant, whom he himself had elevated to that dignity. All Wallachia was conquered and laid waste. Mahomet appointed a new prince, who engaged to pay him a yearly tribute of ten thousand ducats. The same year the Sultan conquered the island of Lesbos, and the following year he reduced Bosnia to a Turkish province. Mahomet, after having successfully fought against the prince of Caramania, returned to his own dominions, and availed himself of the period of peace which succeeded his last expeditions to increase his naval forces, and to complete the construction of the new palace at Constantinople. It bore this inscription: "May God eternise the glory of the Master! God consolidate its construction! God strengthen its foundations!"

Mahomet had no more uncompromising enemies than

Venetians; he resolved to reduce their power, and sent a fleet to achieve the conquest of Negropont. After a sanguinary and protracted resistance, this luxurious, rich, and fertile island fell into the power of the Turks. The year 1470 was employed in continuing the course of his conquests in Asia. While the Ottoman empire was extending its limits to the west and south, as far as Armenia and Caramania, every where gaining battles and capturing fortresses, it was no less successful to the north and east. Its arms prevailed in Hungary and Croatia, and its victorious legions returned loaded with booty. The Turkish cavalry overran Croatia, Styria, Carniola, and Carinthia; and these incursions were renewed every year, to the terror of the inhabitants, and the ruin and desolation of the country. In 1471, this branch of the Ottoman troops covered all Croatia with fire and blood, carried off the cattle, and conducted into slavery more than 20,000 persons; Carinthia and Carniola underwent the same fate. The new prince of Moldavia having refused, in 1475, to pay the annual tribute to the Sultan, Soliman Pacha invaded the principality at the head of 100,000 men; but his army suffered a terrible discomfiture at the hands of prince Etiénne. Only a small number of Turks succeeded in making their escape; and the new forts on the Danube, which had fallen into the power of Mahomet, were again retaken by their legitimate master. While this unfortunate campaign was in progress, a fleet sailed from Constantinople to the sea of Azof, where the Sultan had projected the conquest of the strong forts which the Genoese possessed upon the coast and in the Crimea. Caffa was the emporium of Genoese commerce in the Black Sea. The Turkish fleet cast anchor under its walls, and immediately commenced a bombardment, which lasted until the place was reduced to ruins. Forty thousand of its inhabitants were transported to Constantinople, as colonists, and fourteen thousand young Genoese were incorporated in the corps of Janissaries. A general sack followed, and the booty was immense.

After the affair of Caffa, Azof and several other strong fortresses surrendered without a struggle. The whole of the Crimea itself soon after submitted to the Ottoman yoke. Mahomet was now the more eager to repair to Moldavia, in order to avenge the check which his army had there met with. A decisive battle took place the 26th of July, 1476, in which the Sultan commanded in person, and which resulted in a glorious victory to the Turks. Since the capture of Constantinople, an alternating series of hostilities and truces had taken place between the Sultan and the knights of the order of St. John of Jerusalem, the confederated defenders of the outposts of Christendom in the Mediterranean. The successive wars which Mahomet had to sustain, for a long time protected Rhodes against the ambitious projects of that monarch. But as soon as peace was concluded between the Porte and Venice, the Grand Master took every precaution against an attack, which he foresaw could not be very remote. He summoned all the members of the order to the defence of Rhodes; peace was made with the Bey of Tunis and the Sultan of Egypt; immense stores of provisions were accumulated; and when the Turkish admiral, with a fleet of 160 vessels, appeared before the place on the 23d of May, he found it fully prepared for defence.

Notwithstanding the assistance of a Christian renegade, who, introducing himself within the town under a pretended contrition for his apostacy, traitorously assisted the besiegers, they were unable to intimidate the garrison. The ditches, which by day were filled with stones by the Turkish soldiers, were emptied at night by the knights. An enormous machine, called the *tribute*, sent back to the Ottomans the immense stone balls which they fired from their heavy pieces of ordnance. The besiegers having refused to capitulate to force, or to mild treaty propositions, the Pasha resolved upon a general attack. As a firmer assurance of success, he reluctantly promised the pillage of the city to his troops; but on the 28th of July, 1480, in the midst of the storming, this seductive promise was withdrawn. As soon as the announcement was made, the ardor of the besiegers was extinguished; the knights retook the positions which they had lost, and the Turks, abandoning their standards, fled on all sides, and Rhodes was saved.

This ambitious sovereign was contemplating a new expedition into Asia, when he was suddenly struck with death on the 3rd of May, 1481. The conquest of the eastern empire, and of that of Trebizond, of more than two hundred towns, and seven kingdoms, have given to Sultan Mahomet the Second, an incontestable right to the surname of *Fatyh*, or Conqueror, decreed to him by his contemporaries, and confirmed by posterity. It is the duty of impartial history to judge alike his vices and his virtues, his unbridled voluptuousness, his magnanimity, his crimes, and the wise institutions which he founded. The fratricide which marked his accession to the throne, the heads which he severed, and the members that he sawed asunder, the emperors and kings he perfidiously assassinated, such as the Greek imperial family of Trebizond, the king of Bosnia, and the princes of Lesbos and

Athens, sufficiently attest his thirst of blood. The flower of the nobility of the conquered towns, and the male children of the patricians of Venice, Greece, Servia, Wallachia, and Genoa, were condemned to the service of his antechamber, which sometimes conducted to elevated military rank, and the dignity of prince; but more frequently to misfortune and death. It was thus that the favorites Mahmoud Pasha, and Soliman Pasha, became vizirs. Resistance to the licentious passions of the Sultan was punished with death; the noble daughter of Erizzo, upon the conquest of Negropont, and the sons of the Grand Duke Wotaras, at the taking of Constantinople, died victims of their faith and virtue.

The efforts of Sultan Mahomet to consolidate, by permanent institutions, the empire which he had enlarged by his conquests, his solicitude for the organization of schools, the enlightened protection which he granted to men of letters, and the creation of establishments of beneficence, justify his claims to consideration as an enlightened statesman. A finished education had given him a taste for literature; and his own productions have procured him an honorable position among the Ottoman poets. He granted numerous pensions to native and foreign poets; and his court was surrounded by a distinguished array of profound legists. Under his reign, the office of preceptor of the Sultan became a fixed post. Twelve celebrated *savants* succeeded each other in this employment, from the youth to the death of Mahomet. He constructed vast ranges of bazaars, raised the magnificent palace upon the Seraglio point, which to this day forms one of the most imposing features in the external view of Constantinople; and secured the approaches to the city, from the Archipelago, by the erection of the famous castles of

Europe and Asia on the Dardanelles, where the strait is only 1500 yards wide. Eight of the principal churches were converted into mosques, and four new ones were built. The most elegant of the latter is that of the Fethyie, or the Conqueror, upon the gateway of which are engraved the words of Mahomet the prophet: "They will take Constantinople; and happy the prince, happy the army, which shall achieve its conquest!"

Let us now pass to the institutions of Mahomet, which subsequently formed the basis of the Turkish government. With the Orientals, the state is a house, or a perfect tent; and the idea which they have formed of it, has produced names for the different branches of administration, of corresponding harmony. The social and political edifice rests upon religious laws (Scheri), precedents and traditions (Audet), and the ordinances of absolute power.

The door (*la porte*), first strikes the eye in a house. It is used to designate the government, an expression which is derived from the practice pursued by the ancient kings, of administering justice before the gates of their palaces. The body-guard were formerly stationed before the gate of the palace; and access to the imperial residence of Constantine could only be gained by passing through this body, generally about seven in number. The *porte* signifies not only the government—*Sublime Porte*—but also, in particular, the army. The third figurative meaning of *Porte* refers especially to the court and harem, which is called the house or gate of felicity (Dari); while the *porte* of the government is named the Sublime Porte of the empire. The latter conducts to the edifice assigned to the different branches of administration, where the Grand Vizir presides. In the interior of the royal palace is the treasury chamber; and in the great hall the sofa, or *diván*, upon which the high functionaries of the empire take their seats when councils of state are summoned.

The *Canun*, or fundamental law of the empire, controls the political organization, and divides the functions of the court and state into four, because four columns or props support a tent, and of the fact of the four caliphs of the prophet, and the four companions in arms of Osman, the founder of the dynasty. The number four is sacred among Orientals ; four angels, according to the Koran, sustain the throne of God, and four winds blow from the four cardinal points. The vizirs form the first column of the empire; whence their name, *bearer of burdens*, because the burden of state rests upon their shoulders. The first of the vizirs, the grand vizir, is the living image of the Sultan; his depository of unlimited power; his omnipotent representative, and the centre and pivot of the government. Since Mahomet II., the affairs of the Divan have been almost exclusively conducted by the grand vizir. The *Canun* regulates the rank of the different orders, secular and ecclesiastical, the periodical ceremonies and fêtes, and the succession to the throne. It expressly authorises fratricide in the imperial family for state reasons, and even fixes the degree of compensation for certain crimes committed by superior order.

II. BAJAZET II. SELIM-SOLIMAN, THE GREAT.

The death of Sultan Mahomet was, by order of the grand vizir, concealed until the arrival of his successor at Constantinople. The eldest of the princes, Bajazet, was governor of Amasia; but he immediately set out for the capital when advised of the death of his father. The grand vizir had endeavored to transfer the crown from its legitimate heir to the youngest son; but he was defeated in his aims by a revolt of the Janissaries. For this successful interposition in his behalf, the Janissaries demanded of the new Sultan, upon his entrance into the capital, an increase of pay. His assent gave rise to similar demands on such occasions for three successive centuries.

The war with Dalmatia and Hungary was renewed; and in 1484, Moldavia was invaded with signal success. In 1495, the Czar Iwan III. negotiated an advantageous treaty of commerce with the Sultan. Hostilities broke out again between the Porte and Venice, which resulted in the loss of Lepanto to the latter, and the defeat of their fleet off the island of Sapienza. Hungary, the Pope, France, and Spain, all united to defend the Republic against its apprehended destruction by the Ottomans. Gonsalvo de Cordova ravaged the coasts of Asia Minor, and the vessels of the Pope the Turkish islands of the archipelago; while the French made a descent upon Mytilene. The war with Venice and Hungary, combined with an invasion on the part of Persia, induced the Sultan to conclude a peace with the Republic, and a truce of seven years with Hungary. A violent earthquake on the 14th of September, 1509, threw down 1700 houses, 109 mosques, and a great part of the walls of the Seraglio and the city. For forty-five successive days the shocks continued with such force, that the Sultan was obliged to abandon his palace for a tent in the open air.

On the 25th of April, 1512, the Janissaries, the Spahis, and the people of Constantinople, revolted; and, with the vizirs at their head, repaired in serried array to the Seraglio, where the Sultan received them seated upon his throne. In reply to his inquiry as to their wishes, they cried out with one voice: "Our Padischa is old and sick; we want Selim for Sultan." Twelve thousand Janissaries sustained this demand with a cry of war, and only ceased when Bajazet pronounced these words: "I abdicate in favor of my son, Selim; may God bless him!" Shouts of Allah-Kerim (God is great,) resounded through the halls of the palace. After consigning the imperial insignia to Selim with his own hand, Bajazet died a few days subsequently, at a distance from the capital. Bajazet was humane in character, fond of retirement, with a taste for philosophy and the arts. He followed with great zeal the example of his illustrious father, in the construction of works of public utility, and the patronage of men of science.

Selim was none the less esteemed by the Janissaries because of his cruelty. The first act of his administration was the murder of his brothers and nephews. He engaged in war with Persia, which he effectually humbled by the decisive victory of Tauris. A revolt of the Janissaries recalled him to the capital; he repressed it with firm severity by the execution of the rebellious chiefs. He achieved the conquest of Egypt by a persevering expenditure of blood and money, and the exercise of the most bloody cruelties upon the Mamelukes. His reign of eight years, which terminated in 1520, was one of the most sanguinary that has ever deformed the page of history.

His son, Soliman the Great, succeeded him. The commencement of his reign was happily marked by the restoration to liberty of 600 Egyptians, whom his father Selim had torn from their native country, and reduced to slavery at Constantinople. In 1521, he undertook a campaign against Belgrade, and obtained possession of it. He then returned to Constantinople, and assiduously devoted himself to the affairs of government. The island of Rhodes was a constant source of annoyance to the Sultan, and the more so, because it menaced the new conquest of Egypt. On the 28th of July, 1522, Soliman landed in this hitherto impregnable island, under the fire of an invincible artillery. The seven bastions of the city were defended by the knights of eight Christian nations. On several occasions, the besiegers were repulsed, and in a desperate assault on the 24th of September, they lost 15,000 men. On the 21st of December, the place being no longer tenable, was surrendered by the grand master on honorable terms of capitulation. This memorable siege lasted five months, with a loss to the Turks of 100,000 men, and was marked by the most brilliant feats of courage on the part of its chivalric defenders. Upon the fall of Rhodes, the neighboring islands also submitted to the Turkish yoke. The next achievement of the Sultan was the ultimate conquest of the Crimea. Since the capture of Belgrade, Hungary and Croatia were constantly exposed to the invasions of the Turks. In 1524, Soliman again entered Hungary, and after a decisive victory near Mohacs, appeared before the capital of the kingdom, the keys of which were delivered to him by the magnates. The country was desolated by fire and sword to the walls of Raab, and upwards of 200,000 of the inhabitants perished.

In 1529, the Sultan put himself at the head of his army, and took possession of Bude; the advance squadrons of his light cavalry arrived before the walls of Vienna the following autumn, and were soon followed by the Sultan, who established his camp before the capital of the Austrian empire. After a fruitless series of attacks, and fearing that his retreat would be impeded by the autumnal rains, the Sultan raised the siege, and retired, with no other satisfaction than that of having pillaged the country. For the first time the Turkish arms had received a severe check, in a contest with Christian powers. In 1530, while the Austrian envoys were negotiating the terms of peace at Constantinople, hostilities were renewed with Hungary. In the spring of 1532, Soliman marched against Charles Vth and Germany, with an army of 200,000 men. After failing to take the fortified town of Guens, the devastating army traversed Styria and entrenched itself on the Danube, where the Sultan received and accepted propositions of peace from Charles the Fifth.

Upon his return to his kingdom, Soliman turned his arms against Persia, and after several preceding victories, Bagdad, with all its treasures, fell into his hands. This expedition was followed by another against Venice, in which, although baffled in a siege of Corfu, he fully succeeded against other of the Venetian islands. Prince Peter Raresch of Moldavia was next attacked, and, notwithstanding the support which the Khan of Crimea lent him, the Sultan took Jassy, and the capital of the principality, Suczava, with all the secret hoards of gold belonging to the Waiwode.

The incorporation of the greatest part of Hungary with the Ottoman empire, and the abandonment of Upper Hungary to Austria for an annual tribute, was the cause of the perpetual struggle between the civilizing spirit of that kingdom and the barbarism of the Porte. In 1541, Soliman again invaded Hungary, took Bude, and returned to Constantinople. After various intervening conflicts, a treaty of peace between the Sultan and Charles the

Fifth, for a time put an end to the evils of war. The truce was not of long duration, however, for Persia was again invaded, as well as Transylvania. Both countries, after a protracted resistance, were thoroughly subdued by the victorious arms of the Sultan. The remaining years of this martial reign were occupied in an unsuccessful expedition against the Knights of St. John, at Malta, and in a war with Hungary, in which the Sultan was engaged at the time of his death, September 6, 1566. Soliman lived in an age fruitful in great sovereigns, and he was not an unworthy rival of his contemporaries, Henry VIII., of England, Francis I., Charles Vth, and Leo Xth. He was not only one of the most distinguished warriors of the Osmanic dynasty, but also an enlightened legislator. The superb mosque of the Suleimane was his work, as well as a large number of aqueducts, fountains, bridges, and fortifications. The important changes which he introduced into the laws, fully entitle him to his appellation of *the great legislator.*

Selim II., who succeeded Soliman, upon his accession to the throne, after settling a treaty of peace with the Emperor Maximilian, marched to Arabia, and secured the subjection of that country by the conquest of the Yemen. In 1571, during a war against Venice, he took the important island of Cyprus; but on the 7th of October of that year, the maritime power of the empire was shaken to its base by the naval combat of Lepanto. On that day, the combined Christian fleet, under the command of Don John of Austria, consisting of more than two hundred Spanish, Venetian, and Roman vessels, encountered the Ottoman force of three hundred sail in the Gulf of Lepanto. After a fierce conflict of two hours, the victory declared for the allies, with a loss of fifteen galleys and 8000 men, and twenty-nine nobles of the first Venetian families. Cervantes, the author of Don Quixote, who had greatly distinguished himself by his valor, lost an arm in this battle. The Turkish loss was immense; 30,000 Ottomans perished, and two hundred and twenty-four vessels were destroyed; four hundred cannon, and three thousand prisoners, with a great number of standards, were taken; and fifteen thousand Christians were delivered from captivity. But forty Turkish galleys were saved of all this great fleet. This celebrated sea fight produced a profound sensation throughout Christendom. An annual festival was instituted for its perpetual commemoration in Venice, and thanksgivings were offered in all the churches of Rome.

The shores of the Mediterranean were, for a time, relieved from the piratical incursions which in the preceding reign, under the celebrated Turkish admiral Barbarossa, had spread terror and rapine from the Dardanelles to the straits of Gibraltar. Great as was the humiliation of the Sultan, he, nevertheless, in sixteen months more was enabled to set afloat a naval force of 250 sail, which successfully engaged the Venetians on several occasions. In consequence of divisions with her allies, Venice, in 1573, again signed articles of peace with the Porte. Sultan Selim was the least distinguished of the descendants of Osman, and was the first among them who surrendered himself to all the excesses of the effeminate life of the Seraglio. In consequence of his voluptuous tastes, he ceased to command his armies in person; an example which was imitated by his successors, and has, no doubt, been the main cause of the decay of the hitherto warlike spirit of the nation. His inordinate passion for wine, his licentiousness, and debility of mind and character, corrupted the sentiment of the whole empire. In this degenerate reign, the Ottoman power reached its culminating point, and henceforward its decline is steady and irresistible.

Amurat III., who next ascended the throne, was a weak and effeminate prince, entirely controlled by his wives and the grand vizir. During his reign the demoralization of the empire constantly increased. The corruption and venality of all the public officers, the disorder in the army, and the scarcity of a circulating medium, were all fruits of this epoch, and produced dissension in the divan itself. The Spahis rose in open revolt against the Sultan, who, to pacify the army, declared war against Poland, as well as Bosnia and Hungary; the invasions of all which were repelled—victory seemed to have deserted the Ottoman banner. Amurat died in 1595. Under his reign the Turkish empire yet possessed forty pachalics, and four great tributary countries. Of these pachalics, eight were in Europe and Hungary: Bosnia, Semendria, Roumelia, Caffa, Temeswar, Candia, and the Archipelago, to the latter of which also belonged the Morea, Lepanto, and Nicodemia. In Africa were the four pachalics of Egypt, Algiers, Tunis, and Tripoli; in Asia there were eight. The four tributary countries were Moldavia, Wallachia, Transylvania, and Ragusa.

The death of Amurat was also concealed at Constantinople; but this was the last occasion on which resort was had to this stratagem; for he was the last prince who was residing at a distance from the capital on the death of the Sultan. From this period all the heirs of the crown were kept in close confinement until their accession — an unnatural custom, which has precipitated the ruin of the empire. Of the 102 children of Amurat, 27 daughters and 20 sons survived him; nineteen of the latter of whom were murdered in conformity to the law of succession.

Mahomet III., yet reeking with the blood of his brothers, took the throne. To suppress an insurrection of the Janissaries, they were dispatched to the banks of the Danube. Disaster seemed to throng upon disaster to the Turks; they lost Gran, and the only conquest they made was that of Erlau; which, however, was soon after followed by a complete defeat at the hands of the Austrians. The reign of Mahomet III. was a continued succession of hostilities down to his death in 1603. One of the most calamitous epochs in Ottoman history, it was, nevertheless, distinguished by the flourishing state of literature and legal science, and the rigid enforcement of the laws of Islamism. Ahmed I., his eldest son, followed him. In 1606 he terminated the war which was desolating Europe, by a treaty of peace, the necessity of which was another conclusive sign that the once formidable Ottoman power was broken.

Under this reign the use of tobacco was first introduced into Turkey. The Hollanders, who for some time had divided the trade of the Levant with the Venetians, made the Ottomans acquainted with this new source of enjoyment in 1605. They surrendered themselves with such passionate delight to its use, that the mufti, believing they saw in its effects some resemblance to the intoxication produced by wine, issued a severe edict against the innovation. This proceeding aroused the whole population. It was insisted that as tobacco was not prohibited by Mahomet, the mufti had no right to be more severe than the prophet himself. These murmurs were followed by an insurrection of the people, the troops, and the officers of the Seraglio; and the mufti was obliged to revoke his ordinance, to preserve the public peace.

About the same time, a singular event happened at Constantinople, which illustrates, in a remarkable manner, the charity of Mussulmans to animals. The plague having broken out in the capital, the physicians declared that it was necessary to destroy the dogs, which propagated the scourge. The mufti took up the defence of the proscribed, and pleaded their cause with such zeal, that the fatal decree was commuted to simple banishment. The *protegés* of the high priest of Islamism were then embarked in boats, and transported to a neighboring island.

III. THE SULTANS MUSTAPHA I., OSMAN II., MUSTAPHA II., ETC.

Mustapha, who in 1617, by the death of his father, inherited the throne, was no sooner invested with the imperial insignia, than the report of his imbecility produced his deposition and imprisonment. Osman II., yet a child, took his place. Upon arriving at manhood, he undertook the conquest of Poland, but without obtaining any important results. These repeated failures of the Turkish arms increased the already wide-spread discontent of the nation. The soldiers detested the Sultan on account of his avarice, and rose and murdered him in 1622. This was the first instance in which the Ottoman throne had been stained with blood. Mustapha II. succeeded, but his weak and irresolute character gave rise to new military disorders. Upon his death, Amurat, then but 12 years of age, became Sultan in 1623, under the tutelage of his mother, a woman of masculine energy of character. His government began under discouraging auspices; rebellions of the army were general, civil war universal, and the treasury empty. Asia was in flames, Persia in revolt, and Bagdad, the strongest rampart of the empire in the East, had delivered itself from the Porte. It was difficult to arrest these evils, and extinguish the conflagration. The Ottomans also sustained important losses in the Crimea, and hordes of Cossacks harassed the European frontier. When Amurat had attained his twentieth year, he assumed the government himself, which he conducted in a most tyrannical and sanguinary manner. In 1635, he advanced against Persia, took Erzeroum, Erivan, and Tebris, marking his progress by the most infamous acts of vengeance and cruelty. Amurat returned victorious to the capital; but some years subsequently, being again called to Persia, he took Bagdad by storm, and massacred the principal part of its inhabitants. In the year 1640, death delivered the world from this scourge of humanity.

The reign of the dissolute and profligate Ibrahim was insignificant in it results, with the exception of some advantages in a war with Venice. In 1648, a conspiracy of Janissaries and Ulemas dethroned and murdered him. Mahomet IV. succeeded him, at the age of seven years. Intrigues in the palace, and rebellions in the army, were of constant occurrence. The government was in the hands of women and eunuchs, who ruled as they pleased. Never was the Ottoman court so corrupt, or in such a state of anarchy and depravity. Almost every month there was a new vizir, who was deprived of his office, and often of his life, after a few days of administration; the sea coasts were pillaged by the Cossacks, and the islands of Lesbos and Tenedos threw off the Turkish yoke.

Such was the condition of affairs, when a man appeared as Grand Vizir, whose profound sagacity, and rare force of character, for a time arrested the menaced ruin of the empire. This was the celebrated Mahomet Kopríli. His investiture with power restored vigor to the government, and revived the drooping confidence of the people. Victory again returned to the Ottoman standards. Lesbos and Tenedos were reconquered, and a successful campaign was waged in Transylvania. The two fortresses on the Dardanelles were rebuilt, and all the important fortifications were placed in an efficient condition. This great minister exercised absolute control over the Sultan; and when he terminated his career of vizir, after a service of five years, the treasury, exhausted by the prodigality of preceding reigns, was again replenished. His cruelty caused the death of more than 30,000 persons. As a dying counsel to the Sultan, he warned him to distrust the influence of women; never to choose too rich a minister; to augment, by every means, the revenues of the state; not to suffer the troops to grow effeminate by too long repose, and to lead, himself, an active life. The Sultan, upon his advice, entrusted the seals of state to his son, Ahmet-Koprili.

The first act of the new vizir, was the resumption of hostilities with Hungary and Austria. Upon the banks of the Raab, the Austrians drove back the Turks; and at St. Gothard, the rout of the latter was so complete, that the Grand Vizir was obliged to sign a very onerous treaty of peace, which was not broken until the expedition to Candia, in 1667. The siege of this island by the Turks, is the most remarkable in history. It lasted twenty-five years; the Ottoman empire employed, in its prosecution, all its power; and 30,000 Venitians, and more than

100,000 Turks, lost their lives in it. Public rejoicings, in celebration of its fall, were ordered for three days and three nights, throughout the empire; and to manifest his gratitude to Allah for so great an event, the Grand Signor renewed the prohibition of the use of wine, so strongly condemned by the founder of Islamism. Sultan Mahomet had resided for ten years at Adrianople; but he returned to Constantinople on the death of the vizir, in 1676.

Difficulties arose which produced a rupture with Russia. The Turkish army ascended the Dniester to meet the Russians, by whom they were defeated in the first battle, which, however, they soon repaired in subsequent successes, and a peace was again concluded in 1681. In Hungary, Tekeli placed himself at the head of the rebels against Austria, and proclaimed himself king of the former country. The Porte declared in his favor, and Vienna was doomed to witness another siege by the Turks. They commenced their march in 1683, traversed Hungary victoriously, burned and pillaged Raab, and all the country on their route, and under command of Kara Mustapha, pitched their tents, 200,000 strong, before the walls of Vienna on the 14th of July of that year. The governor of Vienna caused the suburbs of the city to be burned. As soon as the besiegers had stretched their camp in a semi-circle over a space of twenty miles, they commenced operations. For sixty days there was little else than a succession of assaults and sorties, mines and countermines. The greater part of the works had been carried by the besiegers; considerable breaches offered them chances of victory, if the Grand Vizir had commanded a general attack; but avarice deprived him of victory, for, being desirous of obtaining for himself the treasures of the city, he refused to promise its pillage, and to allow a combined assault. During this fatal hesitation, Sobieski suddenly appeared on the Calemberg, with a large reinforcement of Austrians and Poles. On the following morning, after joining in simultaneous prayer, the Christians rushed down from the mountain upon their enemies, and threw them into such disorder, that they broke and fled in all directions. 300 pieces of cannon, 5000 tents, and a vast quantity of arms fell into the hands of the victors. Upon their return march, the Turks experienced a series of such calamitous disasters, that the Sultan ordered the unfortunate Vizir to be executed.

In 1686, the new Vizir, Suliman Pacha, took the field against Hungary. The most important event of this campaign was the capture of Ofen, that formidable rampart of the Turks against Christendom. Almost all the Christian nations of Europe took part in this siege, by means of the chevaliers, whom they sent to join the army of the emperor of Austria. The latter numbered about 90,000 men, while the Turkish garrison of the town hardly reached 16,000. The siege began on the 18th of June, 1686; a general assault was repeatedly attempted in vain, for the Turks, knowing that the Grand Vizir was advancing to their relief, obstinately and heroically defended themselves to gain time. The Vizir finally arrived, but he only partially succeeded in his efforts to throw reinforcements into the town. On the 2d of September, the imperial army stormed the place, and after a bloody and prolonged struggle, this advanced bastion of Islamism fell before the power of Christendom. The fall of Ofen was followed by the surrender of many other forts, and in the following year, the Turks sustained another disastrous defeat on the Drave. These results, combined with the loss of important places in Servia and Croatia, produced such discontent in the Ottoman army, that the Pasha was beheaded to satisfy their complaints. On the 8th of May, 1687, the Ulemas decided upon the deposition and imprisonment of the Sultan, as inadequate to the exigencies of the empire.

Soliman II. was called to the throne in the midst of tumults among the troops, which he appeased for a time by large gifts. The anarchy became so great that Belgrade again fell into the hands of the enemy, and defeat followed upon defeat. An embassy was sent to Vienna to treat for peace, but without success, and a campaign in Hungary failed. The Grand Vizir was suspended, and Mustapha Koprili substituted in his place. On the 18th of May, 1690, he invaded Hungary, and swept on with his victorious legions to Belgrade, which he forced to return to the Turkish yoke. In the next year, Soliman died, and his brother Ahmet took the throne. The Grand Vizir, in another campaign against Hungary, was ingloriously defeated at Peterwarden by the margrave Louis de Bade, and he himself perished in the combat. The following campaigns were equally unsuccessful, and civil war reigned throughout all the provinces of the empire.

Mustapha II. succeeded Ahmet in 1695. Immediately upon his accession, the Sultan commenced hostilities, and took Lippa and advanced as far as Temesvar, while the Ottoman fleet obtained advantages over the Venitians, and forced the Russians to raise the siege of Azof. In 1697, Prince Eugene obtained a brilliant victory over the Turks at Zenta on the Theiss, with the loss of their entire camp, 6000 camels, 900 chariots, and a large number of cannon. Two Vizirs perished on the field of battle. This signal defeat obliged the Sultan to think of peace. In 1698, a congress assembled on the part of Austria, Russia, Venice, Poland and the Porte, to regulate terms of peace. By the terms of the treaty, Transylvania and Hungary, with the exception of the banat of Temesvar, were restored to Austria; Russia received the city of Azof and a territory of ten leagues; the Ukraine and Podolia fell to Poland, and Venice took for her share the entire peninsula of the Morea, to the isthmus of Corinth, and also Dalmatia. Such was the peace of Carlowitz, as concluded in January, 1699. The deliverance of Hungary and Transylvania, by the treaty of Carlowitz, from a subjection of 170 years to the Ottoman rule, was a most striking sign of the deep decay of the Turkish empire. This treaty is one of the most remarkable political events of the 17th century. Besides the material advantages which the Christian powers derived from it, it may be said that it delivered them from the moral terror which the name alone of the redoubtable sectaries of the conquering prophet had inspired, in exposing to the gaze of the world the domestic weakness and general decline of this mighty empire, whose incessant attacks upon neighboring Christian states had filled all Europe with alarm for several centuries.

THIRD PART.

HISTORY OF THE TURKISH EMPIRE FROM THE PEACE OF CARLOWITZ TO THE PRESENT TIME.

I. FROM THE PEACE OF CARLOWITZ TO MAHMOUD I.

THE close of the 17th century, rendered memorable by the treaty of Carlowitz, constitutes an epoch in the Ottoman annals. Its history commences to grow humane, and no longer breathes that spirit of cruelty which had hitherto animated it. It is true the throne was, on two occasions, subverted by insurrections; but its occupants were neither deposed nor put to death. Several bloody wars crimsoned the annals of this epoch; but the sombre night of barbarism gradually broke, and such acts of unnatural cruelty as those of the tyrant Amurat IV., the military anarchy under Mahomet IV., and the political assassinations of Koprili the elder, were not again renewed. The rude severity of the Turkish character was mitigated by contact with Europeans, and more civilised principles of action were adopted; the art of printing opened also, to the Ottomans, a new era. The fundamental columns of the edifice of Ottoman law, the military organization of Orkhan, and the canuname of Mahomet, yet existed; but from this epoch, important innovations and changes in the domestic and foreign policy of the empire were introduced, which the exigencies of its condition, and the spirit of the age required, novel and radical as they were. At the head of affairs, as Grand Vizir, was the fourth Koprili, who had grown up under the administration of his uncle, had fought with Kara Mustapha before Vienna, had commanded the fortresses of the Dardanelles, had been at Belgrade, and had earnestly remonstrated against the disastrous expedition to Temesvar. He was a liberal man, of great courage, a friend of the arts and sciences, and a poet of no ordinary stamp. Second to Koprili in the government, and equally remarkable for talent and cultivated mind, was the Reis-Effendi Rami, who in that quality had been sent to Carlowitz, with plenipotentiary powers, to discuss and sign the treaty of peace.

The ambassadors of Austria, Poland, Venice, and Russia, were received at Constantinople with great pomp when they visited that capital, six months after the negotiation of the treaty, for its formal signature and ratification. Before sunrise, on the day of their entrance into the city, the emirs, vizirs, and other high functionaries, with the Sultan on horseback, assembled at the gate of the Seraglio. The mufti, the two supreme judges of the nation, the chief of the relatives of the prophet, and the ulemas, also united to do honor to the representatives of the foreign powers. The Spahis and Janissaries met them on their landing, and conducted them to the august presence of the sovereign of the empire, with an imposing military parade. In order to cement the peace, and to impress Europe with an idea of his riches and magnificence as a prince, the Sultan dispatched Ibrahim Pasha to Vienna, with a numerous suite. He was charged with the honor of presenting the emperor with a number of costly gifts; among others, a rich tent, the exterior of which was decorated with golden apples, and lined with party-colored satin, embroidered with flowers of the liveliest hues; an aigrette garnished with fifty-two diamonds; a complete set of horse trappings, enriched with five hundred and twenty-one diamonds, and thirty-eight rubies, the bridle being composed of a double chain of gold; a pair of gold stirrups, ornamented with one hundred and twenty-eight brilliants, and two hundred and four rubies; a saddle-cloth worked with gold and pearls; together with a glittering mace of rubies and emeralds, and a large number of other precious objects. The imperial ambassador was soon after sent to Constantinople, to convey the thanks of his sovereign to the Sultan, and to proffer to him, in return, some magnificent presents.

In order to eradicate the evil which was consuming his country, Kopríli addressed himself to the correction of the abuses that had brought about the decadence of the empire—the relaxation of morals, and of the bonds of order and discipline. The first act of his administration, after the treaty of peace, was the exemption of the Christians of Servia and the Banat from the payment of personal taxes for the ensuing year. A severe inspection of the Janissaries was ordered. The fleet received a new organization, and the frontier fortresses of Belgrade, Temesvar, and Nissa were put in an efficient state of defence. Despite of this intelligent activity, however, and its beneficial results, Kopríli was soon removed from office. His successor, Rami, inspired by the same spirit of reform, vigorously applied himself to the removal of the evils of the country; but his measures encountering the resentment and rebellious opposition of the Janissaries, the Sultan was obliged to yield to their factious clamor, and deprive him of his office. Partial troubles, followed by open revolts, resulted in the dethronement of Mustapha II., and the accession of Ahmet III., in 1703.

In the first half of the reign of Ahmet III., the Grand Vizirs succeeded each other so rapidly, that history has little else to do than to register their names; for the administration of but few of them was marked by any memorable act. In 1709, Charles XII., King of Sweden, after his defeat at Pultawa by the Czar Peter the Great, sought an asylum in Turkey. The favorable manner in which he had been received, encouraged him in his efforts to persuade the Sultan to form an alliance with him against their common enemy, Peter the Great. Yielding to his arguments and entreaties, the Sultan declared war against Poland and the Czar. Upon hearing of the advance of the Ottoman army, under the command of the Grand Vizir Bultadji-Muhammed, the Czar crossed the Pruth, and entrenched himself between that river and a marshy plain, dominated by heights occupied by the Turks. In this disadvantageous position, the Russians, surrounded on all sides, valiantly resisted the attacks of the enemy; but they were soon reduced to a close blockade. Peter I. would have inevitably been lost, but for the admirable devotion and sagacity of his wife, the celebrated Catharine. While the Czar, oppressed with grief, had retired to his tent, Catharine, far from abandoning herself to despair, took counsel with the general officers, and the chancellor Schaffiroff. It was decided to ask peace of the Sultan; the Czarina collected all her diamonds and precious jewels, and sent them as a present to Osman Aga, kiahia of the Vizir, by means of Schaffiroff, who was charged with the delivery of a letter to the first minister. The Vizir took into consideration the propositions of peace, and notwithstanding the protestations of Poniatowski and the khan of Crimea, peace was concluded with Russia upon most advantageous terms for the Porte. The Czar was, among other clauses, obliged to restore Azof, to demolish the fortresses of the sea of that name, and to deliver to the Ottomans all the artillery they contained. A special article secured permission for Charles XII. to return to his kingdom. The Sultan, at the instigation of Charles, declared the treaty null and void, exiled the Vizir, and executed the instigators of the peace, who were convicted of having received the bribe of the Czarina. In 1712, peace, however, was again renewed with Russia, for twenty-five years. This, in its turn, was violated by the Sultan; and the ambassadors of the Czar were imprisoned in the seven towers.

The Sultan, annoyed at the intrigues of his troublesome guest, sent King Charles a large amount of money, and ordered him to leave the country. This monarch, upon the receipt of this command, adopted the strangest proceeding known in history. With 300 Swedes, some officers, and his domestics, he sustained the attack of 20,000 Tartars and 6000 Ottomans: when he saw his brave countrymen enveloped by the enemy, he barricaded himself in his house at Varnitza, with sixty persons in all, defended himself with an insane, desperate fury, and killed 200 of his assailants: he was finally taken, on making a sortie to escape from his burning house. Some months subsequently, on account of a letter from his sister, pressing his return to Sweden, he left Turkey under an escort of honor, after a residence of two years within its hospitable limits. Peace was then definitively signed with

Russia, at Adrianople, for twenty-five years. The Sultan determined upon the re-conquest of the Morea, entrusted the invasion of that peninsula to his son-in-law, the Grand Vizir, who, in a few months, wrested it, as well as all their possessions in the Archipelago, from the Venitians.

This striking sign of a reviving martial spirit alarmed the emperor Charles VI. into a declaration of war against Turkey. Prince Eugene, at the head of the imperial forces, met the vizir at Peterwarden, and cut his army to pieces. Temesvar and the whole Banat fell into his hands. He then advanced on the fortress of Belgrade; but the Grand Vizir, with 150,000 men, hastened to the succor of the town. After a battle of extraordinary ferocity, the Turks were obliged to retire, and Belgrade surrendered. An immense booty fell into the hands of the Imperials, including, among other articles, 131 bronze cannon, 600 barrels of powder, 35 mortars, and 50,000 projectiles.

The Porte, recognizing its weakness, accepted the offers of mediation which were made to it some weeks subsequently, and concluded a peace at Passarowitz, by which it ceded to the emperor Belgrade, Temesvar, Wallachia to the Aluta, and a portion of Servia; the Morea was restored to the Sultan. This treaty established more intimate relations between the Sublime Porte and the Christian states of Europe. A Turkish ambassador was sent to Paris, and a Prussian chargé d'affaires to Constantinople. The passion for war was not extinguished; for, taking advantage of civil war in Persia, the Sultan marched into that country, a portion of which he dismembered, and divided with the Czar, his colleague in this spoliating invasion. In 1730 the Persian conquests were in a great part recovered by the valor of Nadir Efchar, who replaced the legitimate sovereign on the throne. These disasters provoked a rebellion of the Janissaries, who obliged Sultan Ahmet III. to descend from the throne. The reign of this monarch was one of the happiest in the Ottoman annals. He added the Morea, a part of Persia, and the fortress of Azof to the empire; and by the aid of his illustrious vizir, Ibrahim Pasha, endowed the country with many useful institutions. He repressed, by sumptuary laws, the immoderate luxury in female dress and ornaments, introduced the art of printing, and established four libraries. There are now about fifty public libraries at Constantinople, in separate edifices, or in the mosques. These collections each contain from a thousand to five thousand volumes, carefully enclosed in morocco cases, and arranged in open closets. They are open every day, except Tuesday and Friday, and permission is granted to copy entire works and to make extracts, but not to take the volumes out of the buildings.

Sultan Mahmoud I., upon taking the throne, vigorously repressed the civil disorders which distracted the country; and after a brief struggle, formed a favorable treaty with Persia. Russia and Austria formed a secret alliance against the Sultan, and for a time prosecuted the war with great success; but the Turks, rallying from repeated defeats, finally overcame both their enemies, and forced them into a highly honorable peace to the Porte. By the terms of this treaty, the Austrians were obliged to restore Belgrade, Servia, Wallachia, and Orsova, and accept the Danube and the Save as the boundary between the two empires. Russia consented to demolish the fortress of Azof, to employ foreign vessels to the exclusion of her own in the Black Sea and the sea of Azof, and to restore all the conquests made of Turkish territory which she had recently made. In compensation for such concessions, equal commercial advantages with other nations was granted to the Russians; the free exercise of their religion in the Ottoman empire; and the privilege of maintaining an embassy at Constantinople. The peace of Belgrade had hardly restored the tranquillity of Europe, when the sudden death of Charles VI., October 20th, 1740, rekindled the flames of war. All the Christian powers took up arms to deprive his daughter, Maria Theresa, of her imperial inheritance. Sultan Mahmoud was the only sovereign who, on this occasion, gave an example of disinterestedness, and respect for sworn obligations. Far from taking part in a contest in which he had every prospect of recovering lost possessions and acquiring others, he addressed the monarchs of Europe a letter, urging them to peace, with a proffer of his mediation.*

* The following extracts will give some idea of this remarkable letter, in which the Grand Vizir, speaking in the name of his master, a *Mohammedan* sovereign, endeavors to recall *Christian* princes to just and humane feelings, by depicting to them the evils of war.

"What sensitive soul, what human being, does not shudder at the miseries which accompany war! Rivers of blood bathe the fields; the conquerors are no more spared than the vanquished by the angel of death; hideous, contagious, maladies, following the steps of the combatants, attack them, beat them down, devour them in the arms of victory itself, and finally cast them in the ignoble ditch, where death confounds them with the animals. It is thus that it punishes debased men for having imitated the ferocity of the beasts in their insensible fury. The horrid genius of evil, in uttering the cry of war, severs with his flaming sword the bonds of nations; no more intercourse between brethren; the law of the strongest becomes the code of the chil-

It was not accepted; and the Sultan, not having been able to cause his glorious counsels to prevail, remained a neutral spectator of this long war, which was terminated only in 1748, by the treaty of Aix-la-Chapelle. This reign was also signalized by the rise in Arabia of the reforming sect of the Wahhabees, under a celebrated sheik, who aimed to restore Mohammedanism to its original purity. Despised for his weakness at first, this new envoy of the prophet ultimately succeeded in fomenting a wide-spread defection in the south of the empire. Mahmoud died in 1754, leaving the empire in a flourishing and reinvigorated condition, and with the reputation of a humane, wise, and enlightened prince. The reign of his successor, Othman III., which expired in 1756, was a continued period of peace, but was not marked by any important public event.

In 1768, the Porte, then under the government of Mustapha III., declared war against Russia, on account of its aggressions upon Poland. To stimulate the Mussulman fanaticism, the *sandjakcherif*. (standard of the prophet,) was brought out of the Seraglio, and displayed to the public gaze. The empress Catharine sent two powerful armies against the Turks, and dispatched a fleet from the Baltic to dispossess them of the Morea. To augment the calamities of the empire, an insurrection of the Mamelukes broke out in Egypt, Georgia rebelled,

---

dren of Adam; the blood or tears of victims attest, upon its tables of brass, that every virtue has been outraged, feebleness butchered, innocence oppressed, and chastity violated. In order to prevent the recurrence of so many crimes and calamities, and to accomplish the views of God, my sublime emperor, who is nothing less than the shadow of God upon earth, invites the Christian princes to reconciliation, and proffers them his powerful mediation."

Azof surrendered, a Russian flotilla intercepted in the Black Sea the supplies of the capital, while a Muscovite squadron scoured the coasts of Palestine and the seas of Greece, to the interruption of commerce. The Sultan died in the midst of the war, leaving its prosecution to his son Abdul Hamid, who, on the 22d of July, 1774, signed the humiliating treaty of peace of Kainardji, by which the independence of the Tartars of the Crimea, Bessarabia, and the steppes of Kuban was acknowledged. The free navigation of all the seas of the empire was conceded to the Russians, as well as Azof and other fortresses, and the partition of Poland was formally recognised. In return for these important concessions, facilitating the aims of Russia for an establishment at Azof, and the means of ready maritime access by its southern frontiers to Constantinople, its conquests in Moldavia, Wallachia, and Bessarabia, with the occupied islands in the Archipelago were all surrendered. This peace, no less than the disastrous war which preceded it, shook the Ottoman power to its foundations. It was, moreover, distinguished from that of Carlowitz, by the fact that it was not arranged by the intervention of other European powers; Russia treated for herself alone, and obstinately adhered to the preliminary propositions, laid down by her negotiators.

This dishonorable peace could not continue long, for the Turks were as anxious to recover their lost ground as Catharine was to push her frontiers to the south, and obtain command of the Black Sea. After throwing the Crimea into confusion by her intrigues, she put herself at the head of an army of 200,000, and invaded it. Upon a triumphal arch, thrown over the road leading to the west, she inscribed the prophetic words—*Route to Con-*

stantinople. Austria, with her characteristic policy, took advantage of the embarrassments of the Porte, and conquered the Bukovina. In her sanguine ambition, Catharine already believed in the destruction of the Turkish empire. When, in the spring of 1787, she concluded a secret alliance with the emperor Joseph, in his visit to her camp on the shores of the Black Sea, she seriously proposed to him the partition of the Ottoman dominions, or the restoration of the Greek empire. The emperor, in his astonishment, exclaimed: "But what shall we do with Constantinople?" a question which has since been repeated by more than one crowned head.

In 1787, the Sultan deemed himself sufficiently strong to take the field. He declared war against Russia, and sent an army of 80,000 men to the Danube. The fleet entered the Black Sea. Austria allied herself with Russia, and sent an army to Moldavia, which, after having victoriously traversed Transylvania, took Chatshim, and repulsed a part of the Turkish forces. The Ottoman expedition in the Black Sea was unsuccessful. The campaign closed in 1788 by the capture of the fortress of Oczakow, where the Turks valiantly perished to a man, rather than surrender. Abdul Hamid died in 1789. Under his reign, Russia succeeded in opening her way to the Bosphorus. This triumph was due, not only to the address and intrigues of Catharine II., but also to the great progress of the Muscovite nation in the art of war, while the Ottomans remained stationary in the midst of the general movement. For notwithstanding the efforts of Sultan Abdul Hamid, and the assistance afforded to him by the French officers called to Constantinople, the Mussulman soldiers could not adapt themselves to European discipline and tactics. The repugnance of the

Janissaries to these innovations was so strong, that they enforced their abandonment by an armed rebellion. To this blind adherence of the followers of Mahomet to the customs and maxims of their ancestors, must be attributed the numerous and grave disasters under the last Sultans, and the loss of that superiority which they had obtained over the Christian nations by their religious fanaticism, brilliant courage, and surpassing skill and prowess in arms.

Selim III. succeeded to the throne, and immediately raised a new army for the resumption of hostilities. The Austrians were already on the point of occupying Belgrade, when the Turks arrived before that place; the two imperial armies, Austrian and Russian, effecting a junction, after a protracted conflict, defeated the Ottoman forces. In 1791, a general peace was agreed upon, rather from the force of circumstances than from any disposition to yield, on the part of the Turks. Admiral Duckworth was dispatched, in 1807, to Constantinople, to compel the Porte into union with the allied powers against France. Upon the appearance of the squadron, under this officer, off the Dardanelles, the Kapoudan-pasha sent the fleet out of port, and endeavored to put the fortresses of the Strait in a proper state of defence. On the 20th of February, the English admiral, with his vessels, passed the castles without receiving any material damage, and prosecuted his voyage, until he met the Ottoman flotilla off Gallipoli, all of which he destroyed, with the exception of one frigate. The British vessels, for want of favorable wind, were obliged to come to anchor off the Prince's Islands in the sea of Marmara. The Sultan refused to listen to the overtures of the Admiral, and the latter fearing for the safety of his fleet, from the new batteries and constructions on the Dardanelles, finally weighed anchor and bore down the Hellespont. Upon their descent, the English were severely handled by the fire of the batteries and castles; two corvettes were sunk, and all the vessels suffered serious injury.* This naval expedition, and that directed against Egypt by England, determined the Sultan to declare war against Great Britain, and to contract an alliance with France.

In the meanwhile, the attempt of Selim to counterbalance the power of the Janissaries by the organization of a new military force, disciplined, armed, and equipped like European troops, led to the rising of the former body of troops. For two days, blood flowed in torrents in the streets of the capital; all the ministers and partizans of the new reforms were massacred, and the Sultan was obliged to suppress the corps of Nizam-Djedid (new order), the cause of the tumults. The triumph of the Janissaries was complete. Emboldened by success, the chiefs of the conspiracy resolved to depose a sovereign whose intelligence and civilized tastes were so unacceptable to the barbarous enemies of every useful innovation. The mufti united with them in their plans. He pitied, he said, the unhappy monarch, led astray by perfidious counsel, and whom the prophet abandoned, because, instead of putting confidence in God, he wished to assimilate the Ottomans

* The demands upon the Porte, by the English government, as presented by the Admiral and Ambassador, were the following: Alliance of the Porte with England and Russia against France; the immediate delivery of the castles and batteries of the Dardanelles, as well as the Ottoman fleet, to the former power, and the cession of Moldavia and Wallachia to the second. Lastly, a declaration of war against France, and the expulsion of Gen. Sebastiani, the ambassador of that nation.

to the infidels. Upon announcing his deposition to the Sultan, that personage complacently laid aside the insignia of authority, in favor of Mustapha IV., whose reign lasted but a year, when another insurrection deposed him and placed Mahmoud II. upon the throne.

II. FROM THE REIGN OF SULTAN MAHMOUD II. TO THE PRESENT TIME.

Mahmoud II. mounted the throne 28th of July, 1808, with the determination of prosecuting the system of reform commenced by Sultan Selim. He was arrested in the outset of his plans by an insurrection of the Janissaries, who fired the city in several places, and murdered his prime minister, Moustapha Pasha, the zealous advocate of these schemes of regeneration. A war of continual reverses ensued with Russia, which was terminated by a treaty of peace at Bucharest, May 28th, 1812, fixing the Pruth as the boundary between the two empires, and making the fatal concession to Russia of both mouths of the Danube, with a part of Moldavia and Bessarabia. Mohammed Ali, Pasha of Egypt, rescued the sacred cities of Mecca and Medina from the Wahhabites, and sent the keys of the holy city to Constantinople, with the captive chief of the fanatical and troublesome sect. In 1819, the Porte recognised the independence of the Ionian islands. Ali-Pasha of Janina, in Albania, raised the standard of insurrection in that country, and kept it displayed amid varying scenes of reverses and triumphs for twenty years.

After centuries of submission, Greece began to manifest aspirations for national independence. In March, 1821, Ypsilanti published, in conjunction with Prince Sutzo, proclamations from Moldavia, inviting the Greeks to rise, under promise of Russian aid. At the end of May, the

Morea was in a general state of insurrection; the islands of Hydra, Spezzia, and Ipsara, equipped a fleet of one hundred and eighty sail; a rich Greek lady, Bobelina, whose husband had been killed by the Turks, armed three brigs, and commanded them in person. Patriotic and secret associations of Greeks were formed in Vienna, and all the chief capitals, to stimulate and support the war of independence by men and money. Irritated at these measures, the Sultan caused the Greek patriarch Gregory, whom he accused of *probably* having participated in the plot, to be hung. This murder was followed by like atrocities in other cities of the empire, upon the bishops and priesthood of the Greek church. In December, 1821, a congress, convoked by Ypsilanti and Mavrocordato, assembled at Epidaurus, and promulgated a provisionary constitution. In 1822, in revenge for the slaughter of the Turkish garrison, an immense Ottoman force landed upon the island of Scio, murdered in cold blood over 20,000 persons of both sexes, and carried as many into captivity. This beautiful island, the garden of the Archipelago, in a few hours, from a blooming paradise in the midst of the waters, was converted into a howling waste. The Christian ear of Europe was pained at these inhuman atrocities, and a general sympathy was awakened for the struggling Greeks. Lord Byron, after causing the European heart to vibrate with his lofty verse, in favor of the descendants of Leonidas, repaired in person to their aid, and also a large body of Philhellenists from America and Europe. First among the former, Dr. G. W. Howe, of Boston, Mass., deserves honorable mention for his devoted philanthropy, courage, and wisely-directed zeal.

The limited space assigned to this historical abstract, does not permit an indulgence in the details of this protracted struggle for liberty. Neither ancient nor modern annals exhibit more splendid examples of valor and patriotism than the Greek war of independence, nor more patient endurance of the woes that man can inflict upon his fellow-man. The uncalculating intrepidity of Marco Bozzaris, with his chosen few, storming at midnight the multitudinous camp of the Turkish pasha at Carpenitza, can be paralleled only by the immortal action of Leonidas at Thermopylæ. Themistocles at Salamis did not fight against greater odds, or with more glory, than Canaris and Miaulis in their fleets of feluccas, with overwhelming Turkish squadrons in the Ægean sea. This sanguinary contest, one of "the bloodiest pictures in the book of time," was definitively closed by the destruction of the Turkish navy in the harbor of Navarino, by the combined Russian, French, and English fleet. In 1829, the independence of Greece was formally recognized by the Porte.

Sultan Mahmoud, convinced by the inability of his troops to repress the Greek insurrection, and the continual disasters of his army, that a radical military reform was necessary to the salvation of the empire, determined upon the destruction of the obstacle to all improvement — the Janissaries. In an audience of the chief dignitaries of the government, May 22, 1826, he solemnly announced this intention, and on the 28th of that month issued an imperial ordinance, terminating with the following words: "Vengeance, people of Mahomet, vengeance! Faithful servants of an empire which is to endure as long as the world, vengeance! Officers of all ranks, defenders of the faith, come to us! We must, by a common effort, repair our breaches, and in the face of the world raise up around our country the ramparts of an invincible army. We must counteract the military tactics of Christendom."

By the terms of this decree, all the young men were ordered to leave the Janissary corps, and to be enrolled in regiments, for the purpose of instruction in the art of war as practised by the Christians. In the night of June 15, 1826, a formidable insurrection of the Janissaries broke out; more than 30,000 of them rose against the government; but the Sultan, advancing among his people with the standard of the prophet in his hands, called them to support the throne. A force of 50,000 men proceeded against the rebels, surrounded their barracks, which they set on fire, and consumed the greater part in the flames, pitilessly massacring all who attempted to escape. The survivors were exiled to Asia. Upwards of 20,000 perished by fire and sword. Thus was accomplished the destruction of these insolent prætorians, who, for several centuries, had held the Sultans in terror, and deposed or elevated them at will. The suppression of the fanatical sect of Bektachi dervishes next took place, as well as other branches of the military force that had previously taken part in the tumultuous disorders which had shaken the stability of the kingdom.

The Sultan now prosecuted his projects of reform with great firmness and energy. To save the capital from the frequent and desolating ravages of the plague, he established, in defiance of the Mahommedan doctrine of fatality, the preventive precautions of Quarantine police. He dismissed his ignorant Turkish quacks, and appointed four Germans as physicians of the imperial household, and founded a college of medicine. He sent young men to Paris and London, to be educated in science and the modern languages, for the diplomatic and administrative service of the government. He permitted the erection of a theatre and opera-house in the Christian quarter of Pera: he gave balls, concerts, and *fêtes*, to break down the Mussulman antipathy to Christians, and completely re-organized the army, so as to combine the Ottoman insignia with the more convenient, but certainly less becoming tight-fitting vestments of the French and English troops, and adopting also their fire-arms, discipline, and organization. He prevailed upon the Mufti to sanction, by a distorted interpretation of the Koran, the establishment of lazarettos; and he even ventured, in defiance of a denunciatory proclamation of the ulemas, to offend the Mussulman prejudices against representations of the human face, by placing his portrait in all the barracks. In 1830, in imitation of the custom of Christian monarchs, he made a royal progress through the provinces of his kingdom. Previous to setting out, however, upon this journey, to flatter the popular notions, he consulted the State astrologer, who pronounced the day favorable, and the object propitious to the public welfare. He gravely shocked and offended his people, by returning from this expedition in an Austrian steamboat, who felt that it was both an impiety and sacrilege for "the shadow of God upon earth" thus to expose his sacred person among the Ghiaours. The fanaticism of the true believers was roused to an intense pitch of excitement by these Christian innovations and practices. The popular discontent, as is usual in such cases, manifested itself in incendiary conflagrations, one of which consumed 10,000 houses. To the complaining victims of this calamity, the Mussulman zealots replied: "God is great. Behold what the prophet does to teach the renegade Sultan to obey his precepts, and not to sully the throne of his ancestors by alliance with infidels." Neither the menaces of ignorant bigots, nor fears of assassination and dethronement could swerve this iron-nerved sovereign from the sublime task he had assumed, of renovating the decayed energies of his country, and of restoring it to a footing of equality with the great powers of Europe.

May 6th and 7th, 1828, the Russians passed the Pruth, under the command of Field Marshal Prince Wittgenstein. The Sultan could not think of defending the Principalities, or the line of the Danube; as he had no second army to present to the enemy, if the first were defeated in an attempt to drive the Russians across the Danube. He was consequently obliged to abandon the Danubian fortresses to themselves, and to unite all his forces in the mountains of the Balkan, to dispute their passage by the Russians. The head-quarters of the Ottoman army was established at Shumla, where fortifications were thrown up. The imperial army promptly invaded Moldavia and Wallachia, in which it met no resistance, and soon assailed Braila, on the left bank of the Danube, which Soliman Pasha surrendered only when the walls were dismantled, and the greater part of the cannon was rendered unserviceable. While the centre of the army was operating at Braila, under Wittgenstein, the left wing, under Rudsewitsch, with great difficulty crossed the right bank of the river at Basardschick. General Benkendorf, with six battalions, covered the march of the army under the fortress of Silistria. The plan of the Russians was to reach the Turks before Shumla, to force them into action, and to defeat them completely, in order that, by the destruction of the only army the Sultan could oppose to them, the route to Constantinople might be laid open.

The seraskier, Hussein Pasha, refused to fight; and suffered the Russians, unopposed, to arrive before Shumla, which took place July 20. The imperial commander, being well satisfied that his forces were not sufficiently strong to carry the fortified camp, resolved, after a sharp skirmish, to fortify himself at Eski-Stamboul, and thus cut off the Turks from the road to Adrianople. Four weeks passed without any movement. At last, Hussein Pasha believed the time had come for something more decisive than the trifling skirmishes which daily occurred, without any decisive results. In the night of the 25–26th August, three strong Turkish columns advanced in profound silence, and fell upon the Russian line with the most determined fury. It would not be just to say that the Pasha gained a victory, in the usual acceptation of the word; but he accomplished, at least, his project of dislodging General Rudiger from Eski-Stamboul, and of regaining the grand route to Adrianople.

The Russians maintained themselves before Shumla, especially for the purpose of covering the siege of Varna, situated upon the shores of the Black Sea, to the south of which extends Lake Dwena, rendering that place inaccessible from any other side than the west and north. General Suchtelen directed the first operations of the siege, which made but slow progress. The Turks made continual sallies, and fought from the rising to the setting of the sun, with a lion-like courage. In one of these encounters, Admiral Prince Menshikoff, who commanded in chief before Varna, was wounded, and was replaced by Count Woronzkoff, Governor-General of New Russia. September 7th, and the following days, the imperial guards, 18,000 strong, infantry and cavalry, arrived at the camp, under the command of the Grand Duke Michael himself. The Emperor Nicholas had also arrived at Odessa, and established his head-quarters on board the line-of-battle ship Paris. Thenceforward, hostilities were pushed with more vigor. The Turks, after a bloody and tenacious resistance, were driven from the fortified points they occupied before the citadel; and the investment of Varna took place, by means of the corps of Gen. Golovin, which had been detached from the right bank of Lake Dwena. The Sultan, on his side, had sent 12,000 fresh troops from Constantinople to the theatre of war, which, if they had arrived a few days before, might have been able to enter Varna without difficulty. But when this corps presented itself, 15th of September, upon the borders of the river Kamtschik, which empties into the Black Sea to the north of the Balkan, and seven miles from Varna, General Golovin already occupied the south bank of Lake Dwena, so that it was impossible to succor the fortress, except by a victorious engagement. Omar Vrione, chief of the Arnouts, known for the part he had taken in the Greek war of independence, sallied out of Shumla at the head of 8000 men, to effect a junction with this auxiliary corps, despatched too late from Constantinople. A Russian detachment, sent to reconnoitre, unexpectedly met the enemy, and was destroyed.

September 27th, Omar Vrione advanced to the vicinity of Lake Dwena, and on the morrow attacked the position of the Russians, reinforced by detachments from Shumla and Varna. The Turks fought like heroes; and the Russians, to escape defeat, were obliged to retire to their entrenched camp, from which they did not again issue, until they had received reinforcements. Meanwhile, the siege operations of Varna had slowly but continuously advanced. Yussuf Pasha commanded the fortress; but the captain pasha (grand admiral), who was also in the citadel, exercised the supreme authority. Two great breaches having been made, the *elite* of the Russian troops precipitated themselves into them, on the night of the 6–7th of October, and penetrated to the centre of the city; but they were massacred. The besieged, however, were soon convinced that they could no longer maintain themselves in a dismantled place. The captain pasha sought, as he had once before done, to gain time by negotiations upon a project of capitulation. The season being much advanced, and the Grand Vizir approaching with new reinforcements, every day of delay was so much gained. It is thought that the Russian general obtained his aims by corruption. On the evening of the 10th of October, Yussuf Pasha, commander of Varna, repaired to the camp of the Russian general, and declared to him that the fortress was no longer tenable; that the captain pasha did not think of surrendering; but that he, Yussuf, placed himself under the protection of the Czar.

On the following morning the Turkish garrison passed out of the town in platoons into the Russian camp. The captain pasha, with 300 men who had remained faithful to him, threw himself into the citadel, and declared that he would defend it to the last man, and that rather than surrender, he would blow himself up. The emperor Nicholas finally permitted the captain pasha to retire with the honors of war. The Russians restored, as well and as quickly as possible, the destroyed works of Varna; and the fortress being rendered secure from any sudden surprise, their whole army, facing about to the Turks, received orders to recross the Danube. But one single corps, that of General Roth, remained upon the right bank of the Danube, at Varna and Bazarjik. The main body of the army wintered in the principalities. The expedition entrusted to General Paskiewitch, the conqueror of the Persians, was more fortunate in Asia. By the baseness of the commander, Emir Pasha, the important fortress of Kars was delivered to the Russians, July 5th, 1828. After a bold march across the mountains of Tschildin, the imperial army suddenly appeared before Akhalkalaki, and took it by storm. The 22d of August Paskiewitch defeated the Turkish general, Mahmoud Pasha, so completely, that he was forced to throw himself, with 5000 men, into the fortress of Akhalkalaki. The residue of the Turkish troops disbanded, or were massacred by the Russians. Several strong places, and particularly the reputedly invincible Toprakaleh (on the route to Erzeroum), fell into the hands of the latter. Hostilities continued until the winter upon the elevated plains of Armenia brought it to a close.

General Paskiewitch established his winter quarters at Tiflis. He recommenced the campaign in the spring; and on the 1st and 2d of July, 1829, defeated Haki Pasha and the seraskier Hadschi Suleh, in the valley of Milli Duss; after which he took up his march for Erzeroum, giving his soldiers but one day of repose. This large and important city, in which was the seraskier himself, was surrendered, by the treason of a former Janissary, Aga Manesch, to the Russians, without striking a blow, July 7, 1829. On the 9th of October, Paskiewitch defeated a body of 10,000 Turks near Baibourt; in consequence of which, the seraskier Oglou Pasha, who was advancing with reinforcements, beat a retreat. During these transactions, the news of the peace of Adrianople arrived at the camp of General Paskiewitch, and terminated the hostilities in Asia.

As to the war in European Turkey, the most conspicuous fact was the substitution of General Diebitsch in the place of field-marshal Wittgenstein. The former resolved not to force the Balkan until after having obtained possession of Silistria. On the morning of the 17th May, the Russians appeared under the walls of that fortress; but they deferred the siege in consequence of the high waters of the Danube preventing the construction of a bridge of boats for the passage of the heavy artillery. In the meantime, Reschid Pasha marched against the corps of General Roth, which formed a long semi-circular cordon around Varna. The head-quarters of the Russian commander were established at Eski Arnautlar, not far from the fortified village of Paravadi, surrounded by entrenchments sufficiently strong to frustrate any sudden attack. The Grand Vizir attacked the Russians on the 15th of May, who with difficulty maintained their positions, when General Wachten, quitting the post which he occupied at Dewna, came to their relief, and forced the Turks to retire. General Rynden, at the head of two regiments, pursued the enemy with such impetuosity, that that of Ochotsk was surrounded by the Turks in a defile, and cut to pieces. General Roth deemed it prudent to abandon his camp of Eski Arnautler, and retired upon Kosludschi. The Grand Vizir then invested Paravadi, which is only five miles from Shumla, and which, in case of an attack upon the latter, could serve as a rallying point to the Russians. But the Turks were yet so inexperienced in siege operations, that weeks elapsed without the least progress on their part.

Advised of this fact, General Diebitsch left the third

corps of infantry before Silistria, under the command of General Krasowski, and putting himself at the head of 21,000 men, with 94 cannon, took up his march for the purpose of throwing himself on the line of junction of the Grand Vizir with Shumla, and of forcing him to accept a battle. It was on the 11th of June that the rencounter took place, and that hostilities commenced at Koulewtscha; after an engagement of great spirit, in which the Russians and Turks fought with their accustomed valor, the advantage of the day remained to the former; but they had suffered so much, and were so exhausted by fatigue, that they were unable to pursue the enemy. The Grand Vizir, having his line of junction with Shumla cut off, was obliged to adopt measures to gain the only route that was left open to him — that of Kamtschik. He masked his retreat by leaving his right wing fixed in its position, and by occupying the borders of the neighboring forest with strong detachments. The Russians were deceived, and believed that the Grand Vizir had decided to continue the contest. In consequence of this opinion, General Diebitsch detached General Toll with twelve battalions, twelve squadrons, and twenty-four guns, to attack the Turks; but he only then perceived that they had effected their retreat by favor of the forest and this stratagem. The first discharges of the Russian artillery blew up some powder-chests in the midst of the Turkish detachments, whose order of retreat not being of the best, now took the character of an actual flight. The obscurity of the night prevented a pursuit.

The day after the battle, General Diebitsch ordered General Roth to advance on Shumla. But the garrison was too strong to give any hopes of success from an assault. On the 13th of June, the Grand Vizir himself returned to Shumla. Diebitsch, desirous of opening negotiations for the conclusion of peace, sent the counsellor of state, Fenton, to him. The answer of the Grand Vizir was: "That he was only a soldier, and did not understand matters of state; he, therefore, begged the General to dispatch his negotiator to Constantinople, or to designate a day for the meeting of duly-authorized envoys of the interested parties." General Diebitsch did not deem it his duty to assume the responsibility of such a step; and he resolved to await the surrender of Silistria, before pushing farther his operations. This event took place the 30th of June, by a capitulation, and left the force of General Krasouski disposable for other operations; Diebitsch immediately availed himself of this circumstance to dispatch it to Shumla, while he himself traversed the principal chain of the Balkan with the rest of the army, in order to advance to the southward. All this time the Grand Vizir was tranquilly reposing at Shumla, and only recognized the actual state of affairs when Krasowski had returned to Jenibazar. He immediately detached Ibrahim Pasha towards Aidos, who, by means of a cross-road, was to get in advance of the Russians; but he was met by the corps of General Rudiger, and put to flight. General Scheremetiew could undertake nothing against the 10,000 men whom Halil Pasha had under his command on the route to Adrianople; but the Pasha, believing in the presence of the whole Russian army, spontaneously fell back upon Adrianople. The Grand Vizir, perceiving that his remaining at Shumla could be of no utility, retired, in the beginning of August, with the 12,000 men he yet possessed, into the rugged defiles of the mountains to the west of

Selumio, in order to harass the right wing and rear of the Russians, if they should attempt anything at Adrianople. General Diebitsch, however, marched with 20,000 men upon Selimno, took the town, and forced the Turks to evacuate it, with the loss of their artillery; the cavalry not being able to pursue the fugitives in the mountains, they saved their lives in a hurried flight.

General Diebitsch then advanced upon Adrianople, the second capital of the Ottoman empire, and appeared under its walls August 19, at the head of 30,000 men. Halil Pasha, who occupied it, not having had time to complete his works of defence, was obliged to capitulate; after stipulating for the free retreat of his troops, and that his rear should not be disturbed. The Russian General insisted that the Turks should lay down their arms, and retire to their homes, and not to Constantinople: he granted a delay of fifteen hours for the acceptance or rejection of his proposition. On the 20th of August, at 6 o'clock in the morning, the truce expired, and the Russians prepared for the attack; but the Turks had already evacuated Adrianople, in perfect order. From this important position, Diebitsch directed advanced corps upon Keurk Kilicia, upon Bourghas, and Enos, for the purpose of putting himself in communication with Vice-Admiral Heyden, commanding the Russian squadron charged with the blockade of the Dardanelles; Admiral Greigh followed the coast, took possession of Midia, and advanced as far as Kara Bournou.

When the rapid progress of the Russians was known at Constantinople, and it was evident that the masses could not be roused up against them, terror spread throughout the capital. Despair seized the Sultan also, who, earnestly pressed by his cabinet and the foreign ministers, finally consented to send to the camp of the victor, in the quality of plenipotentiaries, three of the principal dignitaries of the empire. Hardly had they set out on their journey, when the governor of Constantinople discovered a new plot. The object of the conspirators was the assassination of the Sultan, his son, and the nobles of the empire, and all the partisans of the new ideas; and the summoning of all good Mussulmans to the defence of imperilled Islamism. Hassan Aga, governor of the castles of the Bosphorus, presumed chief of the conspiracy, a great number of officers, and about 600 guilty persons were put to death, and the cafés, where they assembled, were demolished.

Meanwhile, the negotiations continued between the Russian and Ottoman plenipotentiaries; but they were protracted by the unwillingness of the latter to submit to the hard conditions imposed upon them by the victors. By the intervention of the Prussian General, Muffling, peace was finally concluded and signed at Adrianople, September 14, 1829. In Asia, the Emperor Nicholas restored to the Sultan the greater part of the territory he had conquered, with the exception of Anapa, Poti, Atchaltzike, Atzkour, and Akhalkalahi, which he reserved as a partial indemnification for the expenses of the war. In Europe, the Pruth and the Danube, from this epoch, became the frontier on the side of Bessarabia; but Turkey was obliged to abandon the mouths of the Danube to the Russians, as well as the islands dependent on them. The latter bound themselves not to erect any fortification or construction whatever there, with the exception of Quarantine buildings; and the Porte, on its part, obliged itself to leave the left Turkish bank of the river without population, for a distance of two leagues from the point where it divides into channels, to Sulina. With respect to Moldavia, Wallachia, and Servia, the treaty of Akjerman was renewed, with an engagement on the part of the Porte, to execute, within a given period, the concessions made to the Servians. A separate treaty was concluded for the Danubian principalities; the most important points were the nomination of the hospodars for seven years, instead of for life, as heretofore; direction of the administration left in their hands; concession of a special armed force, for the preservation of order. Moreover, no Mahommedan was to be allowed to reside, in future, in the Danubian principalities; and all the fortresses on the left bank of the Danube were to be razed. Among other guarantees which the treaty gave to Russia, was liberty of commerce for the subjects of the Czar in all the Ottoman empire. The indemnities to be paid to Russia for the expenses of the war, were the object of a secret article, and were fixed at the enormous sum of ten millions of Holland ducats, (this amount was reduced, in 1830, to seven millions, seeing the notorious impossibility of the Porte to discharge it.) Turkey also adhered to the treaty of July 6, 1827, as well as to the posterior arrangements made by France, England, and Russia in the question of Greek independence.

External peace was followed by domestic insurrections in Bagdad, Bosnia, Albania, &c., which were not subdued for several years. A conflict with Mehemet Ali, Pasha of Egypt, in consequence of his refusal to pay the arrears of tribute, threatened the disruption of the empire, which would probably have taken place, but for the intervention of the European powers. An Egyptian army under Ibrahim, the son of the Pasha, entered Syria, took Acre, Damascus and Aleppo, near which city a Turkish force of 25,000 Turks was defeated with great loss; the campaign closed with an annihilating victory over the Turks at Konieh, December 21st, 1832. The advance of the Egyptians on Constantinople, to which they were encouraged by the disaffection occasioned by the late events, was prevented by the intervention of Russia, in dispatching a squadron to the Bosphorus, and a military force to Buyukdere. In return for this timely aid, by a secret treaty concluded with the Porte at Skelessi in 1833, Russia obtained the privilege for her vessels of passing the straits leading from the Black Sea to the Archipelago, and the exclusion of the vessels of every nation that should be involved in war with her. By the treaty of Kutaieh, the whole of Syria, with the district of Adana, had been ceded to Mehemet Ali, but hostilities were renewed six years afterwards, between the Turks and Egyptians, and on the 23d of June, 1839, the former were again signally defeated at Nezib, near Aleppo.

Before the news of this disaster reached Constantinople, the public criers had announced the death of Sultan Mahmoud in the streets of the capital. This distinguished sovereign, the thirtieth of the dynasty of Osman, died in the 58th year of his age, and in the thirty-first of his reign. The loss of Greece, the destruction of the fleet at Navarino, and the conquests of Russia on the Black Sea and in Asia, together with the great expenditure of blood and money, undermined the foundations of the empire, and reduced it to a state of feebleness, from which it has not yet recovered. The reforms of this enlightened prince were more apparent than real. In the destruction of the Janissary force, so intimately connected by the antiquity of its origin and the sanctity of its consecration, by the venerable dervish Bektasch, with the history of the

Ottoman empire, the Sultan also extinguished the spirit of fanaticism — that all-powerful support of the imperfect work of the founder of Islamism, the legislation of which reposes entirely upon the principle of proselytism by force of arms. With the annihilation of this fanatical troop of soldiers, the passion of the Turks for war — that vital principle of their national existence — was also stifled. Reared in the Seraglio, and leaving its precincts only when called to the throne, his undisciplined and uninstructed intellect disqualified him for the part of a wise and politic reformer. He found every branch of the public service impaired by the corruption and ignorance of the various functionaries, and the military force inefficient to the defence of the empire, or the prosecution of aggressive war in consequence of its anarchial and undisciplined condition. Undismayed by the difficulties that surrounded him, the Sultan resolved to eradicate the evils of the country by the most prompt and energetic measures. Ignorant of the necessity of a previous education of his people to the Christian institutions he endeavoured to force upon them, his reforms were neither understood nor appreciated. His generous efforts to raise the empire to a position of equality with the Christian States were foiled by the exclusive and antipathetic spirit of Mohammedanism, and instead of restoring new life to its impaired constitution, they have only precipitated its decay. The religious fanaticism which gave birth to the Ottoman power is also destined to be the cause of its destruction. The stoic constancy and firmness of soul displayed by Sultan Mahmoud, under the crushing reverses that marked his long reign, his resolution of character, and his expanded and enlightened views entitle him to a distinguished rank among the princes of the dynasty of Osman

—the most fruitful of all royal races in remarkable sovereigns.

On the 1st of July, 1839, Abdul Medjid, his eldest son, ascended the throne at the age of 16. Two weeks after his accession, the captain-pasha deserted with the Turkish fleet to Mehemet Ali. In 1840, Prussia, Austria and Great Britain signed a treaty at London, by which it was resolved that the whole of Syria should be re-ceded to the Porte. Mehemet Ali, relying upon the assistance of France, withheld his adherence to this stipulation, and Great Britain and Austria intervening with a naval armament on the coast of Syria, besieged and took Acre, and obliged the Egyptians to evacuate the country. In 1841, France united with England, Austria and Prussia in a treaty for the settlement of the Oriental question, by which the hereditary government of Egypt was conceded to Mehemet Ali and his descendants, and foreign vessels of war, Russian as well as all others, were excluded from the Dardanelles, while the Porte was at peace. These events were followed by a rebellion of a very serious character in the mountains of the Lebanon, which was repressed by the energy and decision of Omar Pasha, the present Turkish commander-in-chief on the Danube.

In 1852, a dispute arose between the Porte and the Christian powers, on the subject of Montenegro and the Holy Places. France laid claim to the grand cupola of the church of the Holy Sepulchre, the tomb of Christ, the stone of anointment, the chapel of the Virgin, the great church of Bethlehem, the altar of the birth, and the grotto of annunciation. The concession of these demands gave rise to great dissatisfaction at St. Petersburg. To calm the irritation of the Greek church, the Sultan confirmed anew, by an imperial firman, the privileges, rights, and immunities, which its members had enjoyed *ab antiquo.* On the 2d of March, 1853, Prince Menshikoff, Minister of the Marine, arrived in Constantinople on a special mission from the Czar, having first reviewed the Russian fleets at Odessa and Sebastopol, by way of premonitory menace. His demands of a religious protectorate by the Czar over the members of the Greek church in Turkey, were refused by the Porte, as inconsistent with the independence of the empire. After studiously insulting the Grand Vizir and the Sultan, and manifesting a most insolent and unconciliatory disposition, Menshikoff retired from Constantinople on the 21st of May. This proceeding was followed by the expedition of an extraordinary courier from St. Petersburg to Constantinople, bearing a letter to the Grand Vizir, in which the imperial chancellor announced the approval of the acts of his envoy by the Czar, and his determination to invade the Danubian Principalities of Moldavia and Wallachia, in case the required concessions were not made. The Turkish government, in a firm and dignified manner, repeated its former decision.

As soon as advised of the aggressive intentions of the Russian autocrat, France and England dispatched a combined naval force to Besika Bay, near the mouth of the Dardanelles, to protect the Ottoman capital against surprise. On the 25th of June, the Czar published a proclamation to his subjects, declaring that the rights of the Greek church had been invaded in Turkey, and his determination to reassert and maintain them. The Russian troops crossed the Pruth, and took up a position in the Principalities, where they remained while negotiations for the preservation of peace were opened between the four great powers, and Russia. All diplomatic efforts at reconciliation having failed, the Turks advanced their troops to the Danubian and Georgian frontiers, and prepared for war. In October, Omar Pasha addressed the following summons to Prince Gortschakoff, to evacuate the Principalities:

"MY DEAR GENERAL:—I have the honor to address you this letter, by order of my government. While the Ottoman Porte has resorted to every means of conciliation for the preservation of peace and its own independence, the court of St. Petersburg has not ceased to raise new difficulties. It has even violated existing treaties by the occupation of the Principalities of Moldavia and Wallachia, integral parts of the Ottoman empire.

"The Ottoman Porte, instead of making reprisals, has confined itself to protestations, without closing the door to a pacific arrangement. Russia does not manifest a similar feeling. It resists propositions which the mediating powers have recommended as necessary to the safety and honor of the Sublime Porte. It has, therefore, become an imperious duty to resort to war.

"As, however, the invasion of the Danubian Principalities, and the violation of treaties, are the real cause of the war, the Ottoman Porte, as a last proof of its pacific intentions, through me, as its organ, proposes to your Excellency the evacuation of the said provinces; and it grants you a delay of fifteen days from the receipt of this letter. If, during this interval, I receive from your Excellency a negative reply, the commencement of hostilities will be the natural consequence.

"I have the honor to communicate the above to your Excellency, and to avail myself of this occasion to assure you of my high esteem.

(Signed) "OMAR PASHA."

War was formally declared by the Queen of Great Britain against Russia, March 28th, 1854; and immediately afterwards by France. A tripartite treaty was also formed between Great Britain, France, and Turkey, consisting of five articles, with the following provisions:

1. That England and France engage to support Turkey by force of arms, until the conclusion of a peace that shall secure the independence and integrity of the Sultan's dominions.

2. That the Porte shall not conclude a peace without the consent of its allies.

3. That the allies shall evacuate the Turkish territories after the war.

4. This treaty to remain open for the adhesion of the other powers of Europe.

5. Turkey guarantees to all subjects of the Porte without distinction of creed, perfect equality in law.

On the 30th of November, a squadron of three Turkish frigates and two steamers, having several transports in convoy, was attacked at the harbor of Sinope by a greatly superior Russian force, and after a gallant resistance, was entirely destroyed, with the exception of one vessel. In execution of the mutual obligations of the tripartite treaty, the allied fleets of England and France entered the Dardanelles. On the 22d and 24th of April, 1854, they bombarded Odessa, and dismantled a portion of the water-batteries, but without inflicting any serious injury on the city itself. The immediate provocation to this proceeding was the firing on the British steamer Fury, on the 6th of April, while seeking to enter the harbor under a flag of truce. An allied naval force, under command of Sir Charles Napier, was also dispatched to the Baltic, which is only waiting for the breaking up of the ice, to attack Cronstadt and other Russian ports. The war on the Danube and in Asia has thus far been carried on to the advantage of the Turks; the Russians, having invested

Kalafat for some time in vain, have crossed the Danube, and entered the marshy plain of the Dobrutscha, lying between that river and the Black Sea. The issue of this great contest is one of vast importance to the European world; and its solution, in favor of Russia or Turkey, involves the consideration of the perplexing question, whether Russian ambition and despotism, or Turkish fanaticism and ignorance, is most prejudicial to the cause of human progress.

FOURTH PART.

POLITICAL AND RELIGIOUS CONDITION — MANNERS AND CUSTOMS.

FIRST CHAPTER.

POLITICAL AND RELIGIOUS CONDITION.

In our rapid abstract of the Turkish history, we described, in its proper place, the domestic organization of the empire, but Sultan Mahmoud so completely reconstructed its political form, that but little resemblance exists with the ancient institutions. The governmental organization, and other innovations of that sovereign, extended to all the branches of power with the exception of the dignities and functions of the Ulemas, a circumstance which indicates his careful desire to avoid a conflict with this important body, in the prosecution of his schemes of reform.

I. OFFICES OF THE DIVAN.

The offices of the Divan comprise the ministries of foreign affairs, of the interior, and of finance. By an ordinance of March 8, 1834, all the offices of the Divan are divided into four categories or classes, and the titulars wear the corresponding insignia.

1st class. 1, the Kiajaberg, minister of the interior; 2, the Defterdar, president of the chamber; 3, the Reis Effendi, minister of foreign affairs.

2d class. 1, the Tsauschbaschi, marshal of the empire; 2, the Nischandsibaschi, secretary of state, signing for the Sultan; 3, Ewkasi-Humajuni Nasiri, inspector of the imperial institutions of piety and beneficence; 4, inspector of moneys; 5, inspector of farms; 6, inspector of expenditure; 7, inspector of foundries, of cannon and bombs; 8, inspector of arsenals; 9, inspector of powder mills; 10, the president of the chamber of accounts; 11, the inspector of the census lists.

3d class. 1, the inspector of the state gazette; 2, the first member of the council of state; 3, the Mekfubutschi, secretary of state of the Grand Vizir; 4, the Beihikdschi, referendary of state; 5, secretary of war.

4th class. 1, the president of the *chancellerie* of the revenues of Mecca and Medina; 2, the officer of the treasury; 3, the director of the tobacco tax.

The costume of these four classes of the Divan is regulated by special ordinances. The three ministers of state of the first class wear an azure-colored overcoat, with gold buttons on the breast, a rich embroidered collar, a diamond-hilted sabre, and the sign of the office. The three ministers of state are, by prerogative, called *Ridschal*, that is to say, the *men*, or Erkian, that is, the *columns*. All other titulars of the Divan are styled Chodschaginn, that is to say, masters of the Divan.

II. MILITARY OFFICES, OR THE ARMY.

The regular troops are not called, as under Selim III., Nisami Dschedid, but Asakari Manssurei Mohammedije, or victorious army of Mahomet. The troops of the guard are called Asakiri chassai schahane, troops of the palace. The commander-in-chief of the whole army is the Seraskier Pasha, the first after him is the captain of the guard, the Vizir Beglerbeg. The different arms are: the infantry, Piade; the cavalry, Suwari; the artillery, Topdschi; the miners, Laghumdschi; the bombardiers, Chumbaradschi; and the pioneers, Baltadschi. The divisions of the infantry and cavalry are called Ferik; the regiments, Alai; each is composed of four battalions, Tabux, under the command of a colonel, Miri alai. The battalion of eight companies, Buluk, each of which is commanded by a major, Bimbaschi. The captain of the guard occupies the first post at the Seraglio.

The new organization of the army is that of the Redif. There is also a police force.

The actual composition of the Turkish army is as follows: 1, the land force, which embraces the active regular army, nizam; 2, the reserve; 3, the contingents of the auxiliary troops; 4, the irregular troops. The active regular army is composed of six corps or camps, ordous; each placed under the orders of a field-marshal, Muschir; and who, in time of peace, have their principal quarters at Constantinople, Monastir, Karbront, Damascus and Bagdad. Each ordou consists of two divisions, under the orders of a general of division, Ferik. Each division is subdived into three brigades, under three generals of brigade, Livas. The complete ordou comprises in all eleven regiments; that is, six regiments of infantry, four of cavalry, and one of artillery. Independently of the six ordous, there are three detached corps; a brigade in the island of Candia of 4000 men of regular troops, 3500 of irregular troops, and 600 native cannoneers, in all 8000 men; a brigade in the *Eyalet* of Tripoli, composed of a regiment of infantry and a regiment of cavalry, or about 4000 in all; a brigade at Tunis of the same number. Total: 16,000 men, infantry and cavalry. The special corps, under the orders of the grand master of artillery, form one corps; they are composed: 1, of the central corps of artillery, four regiments; a regiment of reserve, and three regiments distributed in the different fortresses of the empire, in the straits, Servia, along the Danube, in the Archipelago, and upon the coasts of Asia Minor and the Black Sea; 2, of the brigade of engineers, two regiments, each containing 800 men.

The reserve, or redif, forms a second army organized with the same number of regiments in its different branches. The regiments are divided according to the localities, into battalions, or into companies, and have complete lists of officers and sub-officers. The last receive a fixed pay, under the obligation of residing in the towns and villages, among the soldiers *en congé*, but not yet dismissed, and of exercising them once a week. Every year, the redifs assemble for a month at the quarters of the ordou to which they belong, in order to take part in the great manœuvres. During their continuance, they receive garrison pay and rations.

The auxiliary troops are made up of contingents, which the tributary, and other provinces not yet subjected to the recruitment, are obliged to furnish to the Porte in case of war. These provinces are Servia, Bosnia, Herzegourina, upper Albania, and Egypt. The number of these contingents is undetermined, and augments or diminishes according to circumstances; they are estimated at from 120 to 130,000 men. The irregular troops comprehend:

1, the gendarmerie on foot, Kavas; the same force mounted, Seymens, and the land militia, Soubechis, in all 30,000 men; 2, the Tartars of Dobrodja and Asia Minor, about 6000 men; 3, the Hungarian and Polish volunteers, 5000 men; 4, the Mussulman volunteers, average number 50,000. All these different corps together make up a total of 500,000 men, which, however, could not be immediately brought into service, on account of the distances which separate the different populations of the empire, and the expense of their previous equipment. As to the contingents, properly so called, their number, as well as the service they could render to the Porte, are subject to great uncertainty.

III. THE NAVY.

It is at present composed of 2 three-deckers of 120 and 130 cannon, 4 two-deckers of 74 to 90 cannon, of 10 sailing frigates of 40 and 60 cannon, 6 corvettes of 22 and 26 cannon, 14 brigs of 12 and 20 guns, 16 cutters, schooners of 4 and 12 cannon, of 6 steam frigates of 400 and 800 horse power, of 12 corvettes, and other smaller vessels. Altogether 70 vessels, manned by 34,000 sailors. There is, besides, an infantry regiment of marine (Bahrié alai,) of 4000 men, under the command of a general of brigade, and quartered at the arsenal when it is not embarked. The staff of the marine is composed of the Captain Pasha, grand admiral, and minister of war; of five admirals, of whom three are in active service; of the commander of the fleet, and the admiral of the port (Liman-Keissi), the vice-admiral of the fleet (Patrona), the director of the workshops of the marine (Iplikane-Mudiri), and the director of the naval school; of eight rear-admirals (Bahrie-mir-Alai), of whom three, with the honorary title of Miali, command the stations of the Danube and the Black Sea, of the Archipelago and the Persian Gulf, while the four others constitute a part of the board of Admiralty. The Mirmarbachi, or engineer-in-chief, is likewise a member of this board. These different officers have the rank and pay of officers of corresponding grades in the army; thus the admirals are assimilated to the Feriks, the vice-admirals to the Livas, and the rear-admirals to the Mix-Alais, or colonels. The commander of an admiral's vessel, in the same manner, ranks with a colonel.

IV. THE OFFICERS OF THE COURT.

Immense changes were introduced by Mahmoud into the Seraglio; there are but two chambers, that designated under the name of chanei-chassa, and that of the treasury; thirty pages are dedicated to the guardianship of the mantle of the prophet. The number of cooks employed in the palace is about 500.

V. THE GENERAL GOVERNMENTS, AND THE FUNCTIONS OF WAIWODE.

The domestic administration of the country forms three classes of officers — those of governor, sandschake, and waiwode. The two latter are, properly speaking, but a reduction of the former, upon whom they are dependent. The present governments are: — 1. Abyssinia and Dschidda; 2. Archipelago; 3. Roumelia; 4. Damascus; 5. Bagdad; 6. Scherhfort; 7. Baffra; 8. Egypt; 9. Aleppo; 10. Bosnia; 11. Ssased, Ssaida, and Beyrout; 12. Tripoli in Syria; 13. Erzeroum; 14. Siwas; 15. Silistria; 16.

Candia; 17. Trebizond; 18. Caramania; 19. Adana; 20. Diarbekir; 21. Rakka; 22. Meraasch; 23. Tschildir; 24. Kars; 25. Wan; 26. Moussoul; 27. Tunis; 28. Tripoli.

The sandschakes are: —1. Jerusalem and Nablous; 2. Widdin and Nicopolis; 3. Tirhola; 4. Janina; 5. Delwino; 6. Awlonia; 7. Scutari; 8. Ilbestan; 9. Ochri; 10. Semendria; 11. Krochissar; 12. Meutesche; 13. Aidin; 14. Bigha; 15. Koisarije; 16. Selanik; 17. Tschoroum; 18. Tekke; 19. Uskub; 20. Gustendit; 21. Persia; 22. Klis; 23. Smornik; 24. Herschk; 25. Dulkagin; 26. Canea; 27. Akscheler; 28. Retimo; 29. Alaje; 30. Gonia. The number of waiwodes is 50.

VI. DIGNITIES, AND JUDICIAL OFFICES.

a. *The first judicial dignitary. The Mufti.*

The functionaries immediately after the mufti are; — 1. *The Scheichul-Islam Kiajesi*, that is, the representative of the mufti in all political and economical affairs; 2. *The Telschisidschi*, the man of the business of the mufti at the Porte; 3. *The Mektubschi*, his chancellor; 4. *The Fetwa Ermini*, director of the *Chancellerie*, in which are prepared the fetwas (answers.)

b. *Judicial dignities of the first order.*

These dignities are those of president, scudur, judges of Constantinople, and mollas of the holy cities of Mecca and Medina; the mollas (judges) of Adrianople and other cities. There also exist judicial dignities of the first, second, third, and fourth order.

The preparatory studies for these offices are made under the directions of professors called murderisses.

The students are named sochta, that is, those who burn with a love of knowledge. When he has passed his examination, the student becomes mutasoun, or a candidate for judicial dignities. The professor of the elementary school is known by the name of chodschou.

VII. THE ULEMAS; THAT IS, JURISTS AND THEOLOGIANS.

The name of ulema, which signifies the profession of *savant*, is given to all the servants of God and the law; and it is for this reason that the descendants of the prophet, as well as the friars, are counted among the ulemas. This large and respectable body also includes the judges, cadis, juriconsults, muftis, the imams, and those who by blood descend from the prophet, the emirs and dervishes. At the head of the ulemas is the Grand Mufti, who, in his quality of first dignitary of the judicial order, presides over the corps of the ulemas of the whole empire.

a. The Sheik of Islamism, or, the mufti of the capital.

The Sheik of Islamism is invested with the first spiritual dignity of the state, as the Grand Vizir is with the highest temporal dignity. He is the grand patriarch, the pope of the Ottoman empire, and, as such, designated by peculiar titles of honor. He is called, "Counsellor of men—sea of all sciences." Mahomet II. gave to the mufti of the capital a more elevated rank than that of all the other muftis of the empire, and the title of Sheik of Islamism. Under Soliman, he became the chief of the whole corps of ulemas; although the supreme authority of justice, he has only a consulting and deliberative voice, but, it is proper to add, that his opinion generally decides the judgment. The mufti, in a word, is the oracle and organ of the law, and he enjoys the highest consideration. The whole empire is subject to his authority, because he is the absolute lieutenant of the Sultan in affairs of religion and civil justice, and the Grand Signor never pronounces a capital condemnation without previous consultation with him. The respect which the sovereign bears to this sacred personage is carried to such an extent, that he rises upon his entrance, and advances seven steps towards him. The mufti has the right of kissing the left shoulder of the Sultan, while the Grand Vizir himself is only permitted to touch the hem of his robe with his lips. He is irremovable. Next to him are the four counsellers of the Ottoman consistory.

1. *The Sheik-ul-islam Kiajossi.*—The attorney of the sheik.

2. *The Telchisdschi.*—The referendary, author of the treaties.

3. *The Mektoufdschi.* — The chancellor of the mufti, and head of the *chancellerie.*

4. *The Fetwa Emini.*—To whom the answers to questions concerning certain points of law and other matters of law are referred. These questions are always propounded in such a manner that the answer must be simply *alur* or *omas* (it can, or it cannot, be done).

b. The Judges.

These charges and dignities are divided into five categories: 1. the grand mollas; 2. the minor mollas; 3. the muffetis; 4. the cadis; 5. the naibs.

1. *The mollas.*—They are six in number: 1. the judges of the province of Roumelia; 2. the judges of the province of Anatolia; 3. the judges of Constantinople; 4. the judges of Mecca and Medina; 5. the judges of Adrian-

ople; 6. the judges of Scutari, Galata, Jerusalem, Smyrna, Aleppo, Larissa, and Selanik.

Molla is, in particular, the honorary title of the profession of judge; the two first officers are those of the two Kadiaskeres, or judges of the army in Europe and Asia; each of these has six officers under his direction.

2. *The minor mollas.* — These are the judges of the small towns of the second order: Meraasch, Bagdad, Bosnaserai, Sophia, Belgrade, Amintab, Kutahijea, Konin, Filibe, Diarbekir.

3. *The Muffetis, or judges of instruction.* — All investigations concerning establishments of religion form a part of their functions, and especially all that is within the province of the authority of the grand vizir, the mufti, and of the rislar agassi. There are five judge instructors: three at Constantinople, one at Adrianople, and another at Brusa.

4. *The Cadis, or judges properly so called.* — These are judges of other towns of the empire; they are divided into three categories: that of Roumelia, Anatolia, and Egypt. Their number amounts to 456.

5. *Naibs, or Vicars.*—These Vicars are only representatives, the substitutes of the mollas and cadis; they form five distinct classes: 1. Kasa Naibi, village judges, heads of a jurisdiction dependent upon a molla or cadi; 2. Bab Naibi, the substitutes of mollas of the first and second classes; 3. Molla Wekili, the substitutes of those mollas who hold the title without exercising the duties; 4. Kadi Wekeli, the substitutes of the cadis; 5. Arpalik Naibi, the receivers of arpalik, or the impost upon barley.

These mollas, cadis, and naibs, pronounce decisions in all civil and criminal affairs, and at the same time perform the functions of notary publics.

c. *The Muftis, or deliberating legislators.*

These occupy a middle position between the judges and the priests. The first of these muftis is the sheik-el-islam, who is likewise the chief of all the ulemas. The empire numbers 210, whose only business is to answer affirmatively or negatively to the questions addressed to them.

d. *The Priesthood.*

The priesthood is composed of sheiks, chatibes, imans, muezzins, and kaims.

1. *The Sheiks.*—The sheiks are the ordinary preachers of the mosques; the term sheik, which signifies an old man, is bestowed upon every man who is distinguished for his virtues and great age; but in Turkey the preachers and the chiefs of the dervishes alone bear it. The former are called Meschaichi Barsi, or sheiks of the pulpit, and the latter Meschaichi Sawiji, or sheiks of the cloister. Each mosque has its sheik, or preacher. The skeiks form but one class in the whole empire.

2. *The Chatibes.*—The chatibes are those who offer up prayers every Friday in the mosques for the reigning Sultan. This prayer and the right of coining money were among the original prerogatives of the Ottoman monarchs. The chatibes yet bear the name of imans of Friday, Imamot Dschuman, as the prayer for the Sultan only takes place on that day.

3. *The Imans.*—Iman signifies chief of prayer, because it is the iman who directs the attitudes and gestures of the faithful by his own motions. His functions consist in making prayer five times a day, at fixed hours, in the mosque, Fridays excepted, when the chatibes officiate. There are several imans for each mosque; the first is the

real priest, and he conducts the circumcisions, marriages, and funerals. A Turk is punished with the loss of his hand, and a Christian with death, if he strikes an Iman.

4. *The Muezzins.*—The muezzins are the men charged with ascending the minarets to call the faithful to prayer in the consecrated formula.

5. *The Kaims.*—The Kaims correspond to our church wardens, and only exercise the lowest functions. The number of priests is in proportion to the importance of the mosque; but the largest never have more than one sheik and a chatibe, two imans, twelve muezzins, and twenty kaims. In the villages, the iman performs, at once, the functions of muezzin, chatibe, and kaim.

e. The Emirs, or near descendants of the Prophet.

The near relatives of the Prophet do not form a part of the corps of ulemas, or interpreters of the law; but the first among them, the Nakibal Eschraff, as well as the chief of the banner of the empire, Miri-Aalem, who are both taken from among the emirs, are clothed with the highest dignities of ulemas. Emir, in its literal signification means prince; and those are thus called who, in Arabia, are invested with the sword and banner. In Turkey they are styled beys. The emirs are found in all classes of society. Almost all the street porters, among others, are emirs; and one of the four members of the corps of ulemas is their chief.

f. The Muderris or Professors, the Corps of Instruction.

These form the nursery whence proceed the Ulemas, all taken in their ranks. The first college or medrece, founded at Brusa, dates from Sultan Orkhan. The number of analogous establishments, and of professors, increased under his successors. It was Mahomet II. who regulated the corps of ulemas, and constituted its hierarchy, such as it exists, with a few slight modifications, to the present day. The following is the order of this hierarchy: the students of the last class are called Suchta Softa; the next, Mind; and the others, Danishmend. These last are not obliged to dedicate themselves to the duties of cadi, mufti, or iman. These colleges are divided according to their revenues, into ten classes, through all of which the students must pass, before they can obtain a place of molla. The muderris of the whole empire are divided into three classes: 1, those of Constantinople; 2, of Adrianople and Brusa; 3, and of the other towns. The muderris of the first class can arrive at the first judicial offices, while those of the second and third must content themselves with inferior employments.

This rapid sketch of the organization of the body of ulemas, may be sufficient to convey an idea of the plan, at once ingenious and simple, of this remarkable institution. It may be compared to a house, in which it is necessary to pass through all the lower stories, before arriving at the top. The ulemas must pass through all the degrees of their institution, before attaining the great dignities; and it may be said they well deserve them, when they at last obtain them.

g. The Dervishes.

The dervishes carry their origin up to Abou-Bekr and Ali, who first, and under the eyes of the prophet himself, founded similar religious fraternities. The "sofis," or mystics of Islamism, appeared in the first century of its existence, owing to the modifications forced upon it by Christian, Persian, and Indian influences. The dervishes correspond to the Catholic monks, and the sofis to our mystics. The number of their different orders amounts to thirty. The most reputable, those whose organization is intimately connected with that of the state, are the Nakseh-hendi, the Mewlevi, the Begtaschi, the Kadri, the Chalwelti, the Rufaai.

All these orders have their particular costume, of which the head-dress constitutes the principal difference. In conformity with their statutes, the dervishes are bound to repeat, at least twice a day, the seven mysterious names of God, which are also employed in the ordination. They are: 1, La Ila illallah — there is no other god but God! 2, Iallah — oh God! 3, Ia hu — oh, He! 4, Ia Hakk — oh, the true of the true! 5, Ia Hajj — oh, the dispenser of life! 6, Ia Kajum — oh, the eternal God! 7, Ia Kahhar — oh, avenger of the avengers! These seven mysterious names allude to the seven heavens, seven lands, seven seas, seven colors, seven planets, seven metals, and seven tones. Sultan Mahomet wished to abolish the dervishes, when he destroyed the Janissary force; but he only partially succeeded in this project.

7. *The Divan, or Council of the Empire.*—The name and organization of the divan, like those of most of the oriental monarchies, go back to the remotest periods of the history of the kingdom of Persia. Divan is employed in the East for the word *sopha*, because the counsellors of oriental kingdoms seat themselves upon a sopha. Let us now penetrate within the great hall, under the dome of which assembles the council of the empire. This divan rests upon the four first classes of state dignities, as upon four columns (whence the name, Erkiani Dewlet, or pillars of the empire); and it comprises within its supervision the public solemnities of the state, the political festivals, and the reviews. The parade costumes of the

ministers and grandees of the empire, derive their name from the divan, and are called Divan-Kurke, *pelisses* of the Divan. The working-days on which the divan meets, are called Divan-Guni, or days of the divan. Upon those days, the members assemble early in the morning, after prayer, before the gate of the seraglio, Babi Hammajum; that is, the gate of the empire.

8. *Religious Condition of the Empire.*—It is known that the Ottomans profess the Mohammedan religion; but it is so closely allied with the state and its political constitution, and it has such a direct influence on the form of government, that it is necessary to give a general idea of its principal features.

The history of Islamism commences with the flight of Mahomet, 622, A.D. Mahomet aimed not only at being the founder of a new religion, but also of a new state. To give authority to his doctrines, civil as well as religious, he declared them the work of God; and it is thus that the Koran has become the civil and religious code of the Mussulmans. Two of the precepts of Mahomet contributed to render his armies so terrible and formidable. The first is that which admits the doctrine of fatality, and causes it to play such an implacable part in the events of life. There was, indeed, no possible danger for the soldiers of Mahomet. Fatality determined everything—they were either to be victorious, and then what regard was to be paid to danger? or they were to succumb, and, in a such a case, every effort to oppose the decree of destiny would be utterly hopeless. In the second place, the remission of their sins, and an entrance into paradise was promised to all who should perish, with arms in hand, combating the heretics. Mahomet depicted this paradise with all the luxuriance and brilliancy of coloring of an oriental imagination. The faithful soldier of the crescent believes that death is but an exchange of mortal vicissitudes for an eternal felicity; and that bright-eyed houris will welcome him to the celestial gardens, where, amid bubbling fountains and groves of bliss, he will exist in never-ending and ever-varying pleasures.

Mahomet inspired himself with the profound truth of his doctrines, and mistook for divine revelation the vivacity of his imagination, and the fervor of meditation. He considered himself as the envoy of God on earth, commissioned to lead his people to a knowledge of the only true God. In the heat of his zeal, he imagined that the book in which he promulgated his doctrines was a work written from all eternity; his followers said that it had been transmitted to him by the angel Gabriel, in the name of the Supreme Being. This divine origin, ascribed to the Koran by Mahomet, was the cause of the faith and blind obedience it met with among the people. Whatever seemed good and profitable to be done, he sustained by a verse from the Koran. To this day, the chiefs of the Ottoman empire have recourse to the same wondrous talisman. When Mahmoud sought to destroy the Janissaries, he invoked a passage from the Koran, and the danger, in a great degree, vanished; for it was confined to a mere military revolt, in which the nation took no part. When Abdul-Medjid gave a constitution to the Turkish empire, he cited the Koran, and what appeared to be impossible ceased to be so. The Koran, as a work of genius, and a sublime poem, unique in its kind, could not but be regarded as a revelation from on high, by a people in whose eyes the poetic genius itself is a divine manifestation; and in this respect the Ottomans have shown a superiority over many nominally civilized people.

Mahomet did not seek to prove his revelation by any other sign. "The wonders of nature," says he, "of the earth and heavens, the plants, the animals, the tempests, the mysteries of procreation, and the Koran, are they not evident signs for him who is willing to believe?"

The doctrines of the existence of one only God, of the immortality of the soul, of the duty of man to manifest his gratitude to the sovereign creator, to accept misfortune with resignation, and happiness with wisdom; to seek to convert the infidels to a belief in God; to employ his intellect in the study of wisdom and science, and of the true, the good and the beautiful — these are the principles by which the prophet was inspired, and which he sought to inculcate in every page of the Koran.

The whole collection of the sacred writings of the Mohammedans consists of four principal books. They are: — 1. The Koran, to which (according to the popular belief,) Mahomet consecrated twenty-three years of his life, in writing it verse by verse, under the dictation of the angel Gabriel, and which was arranged by Abou-Bekr, the 13th year of the hegira, (635, A.D.) and two years after the death of the prophet. 2. The Hadiff, or Sunneth, which is a sort of colloquy on the Koran, and contains various reflections and discourses of the disciples of Mahomet, as well as some particulars on the actions and mode of life of the prophet. 3. The Idjhay-ummeth, or explanations and decisions of the principal disciples of the prophet, especially of the first four caliphs. 4. Finally, the Kiyas, in which are embodied all the canonical decisions of the imans and priests, during the first century after Mahomet.

The Koran is divided into 114 chapters or sures, which are sub-divided in their turn into verses. It consists of moral, social, or religious precepts, and is written in the purest Arabic dialect, and with the fertility of imagination habitual to the orientals. In the preface of this remarkable book, the following passages are to be found. "In the name of the all-merciful God. Glory be to God, to the lord master of all creatures, merciful to all, to the king of the day of justice. We worship thee, lord, and we beg thy aid. Guide us in the right way, in the way of those to whom thou hast been merciful, and not in the way of those who have merited thy wrath, not in the ways which lead to darkness." Concerning the contents of the Koran, it is said in the same preface: "There is no doubt in this book; it is an instruction for the use of the faithful — those who hold for true the mysteries of the faith, who rigidly observe the hours dedicated to prayer, and distribute a part of the goods which have been granted to them in alms to the poor; they who believe in the revelation first made to the prophet, and in a future life, they shall be happy and blessed."

Each chapter bears an inscription or title, as, for example, the table, the booty, the thunder, the prophets, the pilgrimage, the resurrection. In the chapter on the resurrection, it is written, "In the name of the all-merciful God! Truly I swear by the day of resurrection, I swear by the self-accusing soul!

"Does man think that he shall not re-assemble his bones, one with another? Yes, he can join together the small joints of his fingers. You will see the Lord God, face to face, at the day of judgment, as you see one of your own kind. Then will the caller call; let every people follow the object of its adoration. But all those who worship idols, instead of the true God, whether they be good or bad, shall be cast into eternal fire."

The following passage may give an idea of the moral precepts : —

"Oh, you faithful, remain steadfast to justice, when you are called to testify, be it against yourselves, your relatives, or your friends. Remain, also, steadfast to the truth, as well to the rich as to the poor, for God is more than all them. Never testify against what is just, when you are prompted to do so by your own interest.

"No one of you possesses the true faith, who does not love his brothers.

"Actions are estimated by motives, and in everything it is the motive that gives the value.

"Do not count your good works.

"He who has ancestors is, before God, as he who has none.

"Every child is born with the faculty of acquiring knowledge.

"Tell me, says a man to the Prophet, the works which conduct to paradise. The Prophet answered, he who makes good use of his fortune, who serves God, above all things else, who prays, does alms, and performs his domestic duties, he shall enter into the kingdom of heaven.

"I, Mahomet, am the first of men with the son of Mary. The prophets are all children of the same father. Between me and Jesus, there is no prophet.

"Do not name yourselves after me, as the Christians call themselves after the son of Mary. You are the servants of God, and of his Prophet also."

These few citations will suffice to show the spirit which breathes throughout the Koran, from the first to the last page.

The Prophet prescribed fasting and prayer, and the Turks observe this commandment with the utmost scrupulousness. The principal prayer is the Ramaz, or that recited every day, at certain fixed hours; the very instant is prescribed, and the gestures and the posture which accompany them, are regulated by law. God is served as well on the field of battle as in the mosque. Before prayer, every one must wash himself, and turn his face towards Mecca. The Ramaz is preceded by an introduction, during which the most serious countenance is assumed, with the thumbs placed upon the upper part of the ears; then a passage from the preface of the Koran is read, during which, with downcast eyes, the right hand is placed upon the left, a little below the waist. These different gestures and postures, as well as other similar ones, must be strictly observed. Prayers are made either at the house, or more meritoriously at the mosque.

Nothing is more various than the form of the mosques; some are round, others are square, and some again neither round nor square, but almost all possess a large court, planted with trees, and in which is a fountain, surrounded by a basin, for the ablutions prescribed by law. A row of columns surrounds the edifice, and forms the peristyle of the temple, under which the women, who are not permitted to enter the mosque, follow and hear the prayer. The roof is of a cupola shape, surrounded by a crescent, emblem of the Mussulman faith. Around this cupola, arise other smaller ones, for ornament. In every case, the minaret is obligatory, which is a kind of tower, of the form of a lofty column, the diameter of which varies from four to ten feet. The minaret shoots up from the roof of the temple, preserving, at first, the same dimensions up to a gallery, into which access is had from the interior of the mosque, by means of a door, which also must face the holy city of Mecca; from this gallery it goes on diminishing, and terminates in a spire, ornamented with a crescent. The great mosques, or dschiamyi, have from three to six minarets. It is from the gallery that the muezzin every day summons the faithful to the five ordinary prayers, with the cry, "There is no God but God, and Mahomet is his prophet — to prayer! to prayer!" On the grand fêtes, the minarets are splendidly illuminated with lamps.

In the interior of the mosques, marble tables may be seen against the walls, but no pictures or statues, painting and sculpture being proscribed arts by the Prophet. A great number of columns, decorated with lamps and inscriptions from the Koran, are always to be found in these buildings. Although there are no chairs or seats, carpets abound in profusion; upon these the faithful prostrate themselves at certain passages in the prayer. Upon the side of the mosque which looks toward Mecca is a stone, called Kibla, to which the worshipper must turn his face.

In every Mahommedan temple, and below the Kibla, is an altar, denominated Mihrab, consisting of an excavation of 6 or 8 feet; the pulpit of the muezzin is to the left of the altar, and that of the sheik (Knesy) to the right; in the large mosques there is also a pulpit for the chatibes.

The holy temple of the Kaaba at Mecca, according to the Mohammedan tradition, was built by angels. Adam reconstructed it with the stones that the celestial spirits brought from Mt. Lebanon, Mt. Ararat, Mt. Sinai, and the mountains of Hara and Olives. But the Kaaba, having been transported to heaven with Adam, his son Seth built another, which was subsequently destroyed by the great catastrophe of the deluge. Abraham re-erected it for the fourth time, and placed it under the guardianship of his son Ishmael. The Kaaba remained isolated, down to Kanea, a descendant of Mahomet, who for a skin of wine bought the keys of the edifice, and the sovereignty of Mecca. He caused the temple, Mesdjid-Cherif, to be built around the sanctuary. The Kaaba, which the Mussulmans are obliged to visit once in their life, is only open at six periods of the year, the fifteenth day of the month of Ramazan, of Zilkade and Zilhidje for the men, and the sixteenth of the same months for the women. It may be entered from day-break to noon. The door is elevated about five feet above the ground level, and is only accessible by means of a portable ladder. The walls are covered with verses from the Koran, in cufic characters. The Mahommedans believe that the interior of the sanctuary is inhabited by celestial spirits, and that the ceiling is resplendent with such a dazzling light as to strike blind those who should indiscreetly look upon it. They say also that no bird dare alight upon the roof, except a peculiar species of pigeon, of the breed of those which deposited their eggs in the grotto, Ghari-Seior, the same day the Prophet fled thither for refuge. There is also a belief that every savage animal becomes gentle and tame on entering the precincts of the holy city. The criminals who succeed in fleeing into the Kaaba, or into Mesdjid-Cherif, cannot be arrested—a similar custom to that which rendered the Christian churches sanctuaries of crime in the middle ages, and which yet prevails in certain countries, where churches, convents and sacred edifices are considered inviolable asylums.

The most celebrated of all the edifices consecrated to the daily services of Islamism is, beyond doubt, the superb basilica of St. Sophia. It was built under Constantine, in eight years and five months, by the famous architect, Anthemius of Tralles. Its original form was that of a Greek cross, surmounted by a spherical cupola, but in 558, under the emperor Justinian, an earthquake threw down the dome. The architect to whom was intrusted its reconstruction, changed the dome from a spherical to an elliptical shape, and, to give it more solidity, he placed between the great pillars granite columns, united by arches, and encased in the walls. Besides the principal cupola, lighted by twenty-four windows, there are two large half-domes and six smaller. A long and spacious portico precedes the temple. This peristyle has nine doors of bronze, ornamented with bas-reliefs.

The interior of the mosque is decorated with beautiful columns of porphyry, Egyptian granite, and other precious marbles; but they are crowned with ill-assorted capitals, and the mingling of orders and proportions seems to indicate that they are the remains of other temples placed there against all rules of taste and architecture. Upon the interior walls, on large tablets, the names of God, of Mahomet, and the four caliphs Abou-Bekr, Omar, Osman and Ali are inscribed in Arabic letters. A profusion of glass lamps of various colors, mingled with globes of crystal, ostrich eggs, and ornaments of gold and silver, attached to circles, are suspended from the dome. Around the base of the dome are circular galleries, abutting against immense pulpits, whence the colossal proportions of this noble monument may be seen in all their grandeur. The pavement, originally a Mosaic of *verd antique* and porphyry, is at present covered with rich carpets, and no seats of any kind are to be seen upon it. At the top of a long flight of narrow steps stands the pulpit of the

Mufti. A gilded grating surrounds the space reserved for the Sultan.

This edifice, as seen from the exterior, does not present an agreeable aspect from the confused medley of heterogeneous constructions; the effect of the dome is, however, imposing, although, from its sunken form, less conspicuous at a distance than that of other mosques. As a whole, St. Sophia is not so striking as the beautiful mosque of Sultan Ahmed, on the Hippodrome, which, although inferior to it in extent, surpasses it in elegance and magnificence of architecture.

The use of wine, as well as all fermented liquors of an intoxicating kind, comprised under the general name of *muskirat* (intoxicating drinks), are absolutely prohibited to the Mussulmans in several verses of the Koran, of which the following is one of the most positive: "Oh! you believers! know of a truth that wine, gaming, and idols, are abominations suggested by the cunning of the devil. . . . . Verily, it is by wine and play that the spirit of darkness seeks to array you, one against the other." "Wine," said Mahomet, "is the mother of abominations. The moment a man takes in hand a glass of that liquor, he is struck by an anathema of the angels of heaven and earth." In consequence of this absolute prohibition, the horror of the Mussulman for wine is such that he cannot swallow a drop without resorting to some external or internal antidote. The vessel which may have contained it must be washed ten times before being again used. Seadeddin, the Ottoman historian, attributes all the disasters which afflicted the reign of Bajazet the 1st, to his love of wine and drunken revelry. Happy would it be for Christian nations did the same aversion for intoxicating beverages prevail among them!

The cypress is regarded by the Mussulmans, as well as by the Christians, as a funereal tree; with them, as with us, its melancholy verdure is appropriated to the decoration of cemeteries. These trees are, however, much less numerous in our burial-grounds than in those of Mohammedans. The custom prevalent among the latter of placing a cypress upon each tomb, converts their cemeteries into immense and sombre forests, which give to the Oriental landscapes a character of immobility and solemnity in unison with the exterior of the people.

On all sides, and particularly on the borders of the sea, are to be seen these groves of cypresses which, in this luxuriantly fertile country, attain to a great height and size. But of all the cemeteries, that of Scutari, one of the suburbs of Constantinople, on the Asiatic side of the Bosphorus, is the most remarkable for its extent and beauty. It is a magnificent forest, situated on a gentle declivity, pierced by wide avenues, and covering a surface of more than three miles. The monumental stones are all of marble, from the island of Marmora; they consist of a column, terminated by a turban, of which the great variety of form denotes the rank of the deceased; those of the women are more simple, and are readily distinguished. An inscription sculptured in bas-relief, and carefully gilded, denotes the name and qualities of the dead, for whom the divine clemency is invoked. These epitaphs are sometimes in verse, commemorative of the fragility of life, and eulogistic of the being whose loss is deplored. A cavity excavated in the tomb, is destined for the reception of the flowers and plants with which the relatives signalise their visits to the resting-place of their brother, sister, or parent.

The funerals of the Mussulmans are characterised by

a grave and simple character, which cannot fail of producing great emotion of feeling. When the body has been well washed, it is carefully wiped, and camphor is thrown upon the forehead, the knees, hands, and feet. It is then enveloped in a white cloth, covered with verses from the Koran, and is exposed at the door of the house on a bier sustained upon trussles. This exposition lasts for several hours; the iman arrives, throws water on the body, and prepares to accompany it to its final abode, whither it is sometimes carried by friends, or by mercenaries, and frequently by persons who regard this pious duty as an act of meritorious devotion. The funeral procession is composed exclusively of men; women are, however, frequently seen weeping over the grave, who are paid for this testimony of respect for the deceased. The Mussulmans undoubetedly inherited this custom from the Greeks and Romans. When the funeral arrives at the cemetery, the iman takes care to turn the face of the corpse towards Mecca; and then, advancing to the edge of the grave, pronounces in a solemn tone this profession of faith: "I believe in one omnipotent God, and I adore only him. I believe that Mahomet is the envoy of God on earth, and the prophet of prophets. I believe, also, that Ali is the true chief of the faithful; that this land is his, and that the true believers owe him obedience, &c."

The iman then addresses the dead; "Know well," says he, "that the God we adore is great and glorious; that he is the most powerful and the most elevated of all existences, and that there is none above him. Rest assured, also, that Mahomet is the first of all prophets, and the most cherished of all the messengers of God; that Ali and his successors are the only true guides of good believers, and that all which proceeds from them and the prophets is true; that the visit which Mounkir and Nekir, the two angels of darkness and messengers of Allah, are about to make to you is true; . . . . that heaven and earth exist; that hell and the day of judgment are also true; confidently rely upon all these things, for they are true. Now may God thy master, the great and glorious God, who will one day come to raise all the dead from their tombs, be merciful to thee; may he accept thy answers, and conduct thee in the way of salvation; may he grant thee the favor of approaching his divinity and the prophets; and may his grace be with you forever! Amen!"

The iman then retires some thirty or forty paces, and cries out with a loud voice, "Approach, Mounkir and Nekir; approach! behold a true believer; come, he awaits you!" He then returns to the edge of the grave, and says, "Great and glorious God, we humbly implore thee to render the earth light to thy pious servant, and may he find grace and mercy at thy hands! Amen!"

The cemetery of Scutari, which we have just described, offers a striking contrast with that which dominates the quarters of Pera and Topkhane, in Constantinople, and which, under the name of the *Champ des Morts*, is appropriated to the Greeks, Armenians, and Franks. In the former, in which only Mussulmans are interred, a solemn and profound silence reigns, while the latter presents the most animated spectacle. It is the *rendezvous* of the fashionable society of the Christian quarter of Pera, who every day resort to it to enjoy the most admirable view which can be conceived, and of which the spectator never tires; this immense prospect embraces the shore of Scutari, of Calcedonia, the Princes' Islands, and on the horizon Mount Olympus of Bithynia; then the opening of the Bosphorus, in the sea of Marmora, the Seraglio point, and the second, seven-hilled imperial city, with its minarets and domes, the port of the Golden Horn, Eyoub, Galata; in a word, the whole of that incredible array of picturesque scenes, over which a pure sky sheds its magic hues.

For the Mussulman, Scutari is the preferred place of interment, because it is situated on the same soil with the holy cities of Mecca and Medina. The Turks look upon Asia as their true country, and they believe that the ashes of the true believers will more securely repose there than on the European continent, where, according to the popular conviction, the Ottoman empire is destined to a more brief existence. Believing, as they do, that their possessions in Europe will, sooner or later, fall into the hands of the ghiaours, nothing is more revolting to the Turks than the apprehension that their ashes may some day be trodden under foot by the unbelievers.

The exercises of the turning dervishes, or *mevlevi*, are among the few religious spectacles of Constantinople, at which the Christian stranger is permitted to be present. These monks, who enjoy a great influence in the East, admit the public to their ceremonies every Friday. Their principal establishment is in the Christian quarter of Pera, in the vicinity of the great cemetery. Nothing can be more singular than their manner of worshipping the Divinity. The spectators occupy a gallery, which, at an elevation of five or six feet, surrounds the smooth, polished floor, upon which the devotees go through their manœuvres. The superior is first seen to enter, escorted by two brethren, who seat themselves on the sedjeddahs (prayer-carpets), with the face directed towards Mecca and Medina. Next follows a crowd of the brethren of the convent, advancing, one after another, in profound silence. The sacred phalanx makes the circuit of the hall, and each monk, in passing, salutes the superior, who neither responds by word nor gesture.

Thereupon, they all suddenly turn round upon their heels; by degrees, this rotary movement becomes more rapid, and the dervishes diffuse themselves through the hall. Their arms are crossed, the head sunken on the shoulder, the eyes closed, and the countenance glowing with delirious ecstacy. Their robes, adroitly disengaged from the sash at the beginning of their evolutions, puff up with air, and stand out in a circle at several feet from the body. This species of balloon sustains them, and powerfully aids them to preserve their equilibrium. These movements are accompanied with discordant music, composed of ear-piercing hautboys and clamorous kettle-drums. This orchestra, which is in perfect keeping with the character of the ceremony, guides the movements of the turners, restrains or accelerates them according to the prescribed rules, and only ceases when the fraternity has left the room. There is a moment when the music, precipitating its march, stimulates these revolving bodies into an extraordinary agitation, and raises their ecstacy to the highest pitch of frenzy; a singular spectacle, which often gives a spectator the vertigo, and astonishes him by its novelty and eccentricity, as a religious exercise. These ceremonies occupy about an hour, and during all this interval of time, the indefatigable brethren repose but twice, for a few moments.

It is pretended that the mevlevi are the secret instruments of the political police. Their riches, and the influence they exercise upon all classes of Mussulman society, give them the means of discovering what escapes the officers of government, who are always very negligent in the execution of their duties, and but little skilled in *espionage.* The Sultan, occasionally, is present at these ceremonies, and it is said that, during their dance, he is advised, through secret signs and words, by some one of the brethren, of anything of importance that may be on foot in the capital. When the three acts of this curious form of worship are finished, the dervishes again make the circuit of the hall, inclining their heads before their superior, who then rises and retires, followed by the pious cohort. This monastic order, and that of the *howling dervishes* at Scutari, are among the most curious institutions of Islamism.

Another characteristic sight of the capital is the assembling and departure of the pilgrim caravan for Mecca. This pilgrimage, as is well known, is commanded by the Koran, and although, by another article of the holy book, the Mussulmans may be exempted from its observance on the payment of a small fine; they, in general, obey the injunction, unless prevented by some overruling cause, such as physical debility, or sickness.

The pilgrims assemble at Scutari, under the command of their chief, the Surre-Emini, on the day fixed for the departure of the caravan. It is an interesting spectacle, this multitude of individuals preparing to encounter the fatigues and dangers of a long voyage across the burning sands of the desert. Provided with some articles of food, and a small number of utensils, among which figure the indispensable coffee pot, they begin their march, some on horses, some on camels, and others on foot. A remarkable object in the procession is the sacred camel, bearer of the presents, which the Sultan annually sends to the temple at Mecca. Other camels, among those which carry the baggage, are loaded with leather panniers, filled with medicines; and during the journey, they are confided to the special charge of a Turkish physician. The benedictions and good wishes of the spectators accompany the pilgrims.

How many of these intrepid pilgrims will never see the end of the journey! When they traverse the deserts which separate Asia Minor from the holy city, provisions and water may fail them, a consuming sun will inflame their blood, and parch their throats with a torturing thirst; diseases will assail them, which the remedies, composed by their medical attendants, are not of a nature to remove; other enemies no less formidable, the wandering hordes of Bedouins, will pitilessly rob and murder them; a long train of skeletons will mark the route pursued by the caravan, which will at last arrive at the city of the Prophet, exhausted, perishing, and greatly diminished in numbers. But what are all these risks in comparison with the glory achieved by the journey? Are not those who die by the way, assured of eternal felicity? Happy, these elect of heaven! those who survive them, envy their fate. Upon the return, the same perils, the same enemies, are to be encountered; but heaven reserves eternal palms to those who have thus perilled their lives, in order to address their prayers to God in his privileged temple; and the title of *Hadji*,* which ever after is bestowed upon the pilgrims, is a sufficient indemnification for so many sufferings, so heroically undergone.†

* Hadji signifies holy. This title is only given to the Mussulmans, who have performed the pilgrimage to Mecca.

† Besides Mecca, the more devout Mussulmans visit Jerusalem in memory of Christ, Medina, which contains the tomb of the

CHAPTER SECOND.

MANNERS AND CUSTOMS OF THE TURKS.

In eating their meals, the Turks do not take their places at table, as we; but sit cross-legged upon a carpet or piece of leather, spread upon the floor, with their faces turned to the east. A small tripod is placed before them, upon which the meals are served in a large round dish of tinned copper. Each guest has before him a piece of unleavened bread, of the form of a pancake, which also answers the purpose of a plate, of which the Turks make no use. Knives and forks are also considered superfluous. The only table utensils are wooden spoons, ranged in a heap upon the floor cloth. In helping themselves to unsauced meats, the fingers alone are employed.

The principal and favorite dish of the Turks is the pilaff, which is boiled rice, strongly seasoned with pepper. The richer class eat it with chicken, duck, or mutton. In general, meat is but little eaten; and it is always preferred boiled. Beans, peas, and other vegetables, are the more usual dishes. Whey is one of the daily articles of food, and nothing but water is drunk during the repast. The Turks generally dine after sunset; and a considerable number of devout persons make but one meal for

---

Prophet, and the city of Ali, the schismatic, to which latter the *chiite* sectaries, in particular, resort. They sometimes, to accomplish their acts of piety, go into the deserts of Idumea, and ascend Mount Hor, to pray at the tomb of Haroun (Aaron), and then traverse the wilderness to Hebron, to kneel in devotion at the sepulchre of Abraham.

the whole day, at this hour. Others, on the contrary, eat several times, especially after the morning prayer, at noon, when they lunch on fruits, and a regular dinner at five o'clock. The breakfast consists of coffee, and kaimac (a mixture of milk, cake, and melon); sometimes also of sherbet (a kind of very sweet raspberry, strawberry, or apricot syrup). A refreshing beverage, of which the Turks are very fond, is *yaourt*, which is made of milk fermented with a mixture of wine dregs, or yeast, and keeps for a long time. Coffee, however, is the preferred beverage; and opium is sometimes taken to produce intoxication. The public cafés, once dedicated to the consumption of this weed, and where its devotees might be seen in every stage of its effects, from stupid inanity to the wildest delirium, have, within a few years, been closed by order of the government.

The Turkish bread has no leaven, and can only be eaten fresh. Frequently the grain is simply roasted; and is eaten in this state like bread, without any other preparation. The Turks observe the fast-days with the utmost strictness. During the twenty-nine days of the month of Ramazan, the true Mussulman is obliged to abstain from eating or drinking, from sunrise to sunset. He is even prohibited from smoking, or inhaling the odor of any perfume. These injunctions, which are an actual punishment during the long days of the warm months, are scrupulously observed. No one would dare to contravene them, at least publicly; for he would be looked upon as an apostate, and in danger of eternal misery.

During the day, the abstinence is complete; but when the cannon announces the setting of the sun, and the rupture of the fast, the Mussulman indemnifies himself for the privations of the day by an abundant supper. It is just, however, to state, that he manifests no impatience in awaiting the signal, which puts an end to his daily torture. An hour before night, he repairs to the café, or beneath the shade of a tree, and looks with indifference upon the Frank, alongside of whom he is seated, eating, drinking, and smoking. When he hears the sound of the cannon, he tranquilly rises, and returns at a measured pace to his residence, without betraying the least sign of joy upon his countenance.

Meanwhile, the streets of the city, so gloomy and deserted in the day-time, fill again with people, and glitter with myriads of fires. The illuminations of the mosques, the lights of the cafés and shops, and the lanterns of the provision-shops, envelope Constantinople in a splendid blaze, which dazzles the eyes, and covers the waters of the Bosphorus, of the Golden Horn, and the Sea of Marmora, with a golden glow. The Easter of the Turks, or the little *Bairam*, lasts three days, which joyously terminates this long and painful fast. This fête produces a sudden change in the character and bearing of the Mussulman. His ordinarily serious face assumes a gay and satisfied expression. He is affable to everybody, without distinction. Of some, he grasps the hand with affectionate warmth; to others, he proffers his own without arrogance or pretence; to all he wishes happy days, and the felicities of Paradise. He pardons his enemies for the evil they have done him, and he reproaches those who have kept at a distance from him. He forgets his business, and he postpones his troubles to the end of the festival. These are three days of real enjoyment, which break the uniformity of his life.

The moon of Zildigi brings other holidays. Seventy days after the fête to which we have just referred, comes the Grand *Bairam*, or feast of sacrifices (in commemoration of the sacrifice of Abraham), which continues for four days. Then, as during the little Bairam, there is a sincere interchange of good wishes and compliments, and generosity, and oblivion of offences are again the order of the day. The mosques resound with prayer and the reading of the holy volume; the Sultan himself goes in procession and with great pomp, to prostrate himself before the divine majesty. The rich visit and entertain each other in magnificent style; the poor find in the public charity all that they need to imitate the example of their superiors; all Constantinople is in gala, and the paschal lamb is found on all tables.

Hardly have the four consecrated days of the Koran expired, when everything returns to its accustomed order; the physiognomy of the Turks resumes its ordinary gravity; the city becomes quiet, every one returns to his business, and there is no more talk of amusement until the following year. The Ramazan, in the space of thirty-three years, runs through all the different seasons of the year. The epoch is never determined a long time in advance. The phases of the moon, as is well known, regulate the succession of months in the East. Although a knowledge of astronomy is, at the present time, sufficiently diffused in Turkey to enable a few Mussulmans to calculate the lunar revolutions, the priests of the mosques are, nevertheless, bound, as formerly, to pass the night on the minarets to watch for the new moon, and it is after their reports that the Turkish calendar is arranged. But these measures did not appear sufficient for the sacred months. The government, consequently, charges two persons to go and observe the moon of Ramazan from the summit of the Giant's mountain, on the Asiatic shore of the Bosphorus.

The report of these messengers fixes the epoch of the fast and the festivals. When, by chance, the sky is cloudy, or the atmosphere is obscured by fogs which intercept the light of the stars, reference is had to the chief of the astrologists, who solves the difficulty by affirming that the moon ought to have appeared at such a moment of the night. His declaration suffices, and the three sacred epochs are proclaimed.

A frank and reckless gaiety is never to be seen among the Turks. Dances and public sports, noisy amusements, &c., are rigidly prohibited. The popular pastime consists in slow and silent promenades through the streets or in the environs. Parents and friends unite in parties of ten or fifteen to visit their relatives and acquaintances, but these visits never last longer than a few minutes. The Turks sometimes form groups upon the squares and promenades, smoke, drink coffee, and converse upon the rumors and news of the day with an extraordinary equanimity and complacency. A man, perhaps, is passing in the street, bending under the weight of a burden enveloped in a camel's skin, and roughly corded together; he may be asked, perhaps: "What are you carrying there?" and if he replies, "A dead slave!" no one would think of questioning him farther, so utterly indifferent are they to know, when seeing a dead man borne along, if he has been assassinated, drowned, or suddenly struck down by some secret malady.

Some commercial notabilities, accompanied by members of their respective embassies, are assembled in the antechamber of a Turkish minister, on the subject of a commercial treaty concluded with the Porte; the statesman is seated by himself in a corner of the sofa, and while the deputation is explaining the object of their visit, he will be tranquilly paring his nails with a penknife. This important operation terminated, he will call one of the subalterns of the *bureau*, deliver him on a sheet of paper the nail-parings, and phlegmatically recommend him to bury them in a corner of the garden. It is understood that the minister does not open his mouth the whole time the audience endures, and it must not be forgotten that we are speaking of a statesman, and of what takes place, not in Kurdistan, but Constantinople. It is well known that, even at the present day, astrology plays a prominent part, as well in the high government spheres, as in the modest circles of provincial administration; and that no agent, small or great, would dare to take a grave resolution, to set out on a journey, or to engage in any other important action, without consulting the Munedschimbaschi (court-astrologer), and unless he had declared the stars propitious to the projected affair.

After this, there can be no astonishment created at learning that the proposition adopted with such commendable zeal by the government, (the enlightened and liberal spirit of which is worthy of all praise,) of allowing a meridian ball to be erected on the Seraskier square at Constantinople, like those of Trieste and Greenwich, was obliged to be abandoned, the Munedschimbaschi have announced that it would be unlucky to the Turkish empire.

The Oriental poets call tobacco, coffee, opium and wine, the four elements of the world of enjoyment — the four cushions of the sofa of pleasure. On the other hand, the Ulemas denominate them the four columns of the tent of voluptuousness, or the four ministers of the devil. Tobacco has become of such universal use among the Ottomans, that there are many who smoke six, ten, and twenty pipes; there are likewise some who smoke incessantly while their eyes are open. As much attention is paid to the beauty of the pipe as to the good quality of the tobacco. The stems (tchibouk) are ordinarily of cherry, jasmin, rose, and walnut woods, &c., garnished with gold or silver, and are terminated by mouth-pieces of yellow or white amber, and sometimes of coral, elegantly worked. The bowls of these pipes are made of a fine clay, which has undergone a particular preparation, and some are even gilded.

It is a common act of politeness among the Mussulmans to invite every body who visits them to smoke, and it is considered indecorous to refuse. For this reason, a great number of long tschibouks are always to be seen arranged in the antechambers in stands. The smokers sit down on the low sofa or divan which surrounds the walls of the room, with a small brazen dish on the floor before them, upon which they rest the bowl of their pipe, that its ashes or tobacco may not set the carpet or matting on fire. A Turk rarely goes out without his pipe and tobacco; the former is divided into two or three pieces, which fasten together by silver screws, and it is carried in a cloth cover, attached to a belt under the coat. The richer Mussulmans are always followed by a black slave, who is the bearer of this indispensable instrument of enjoyment. The amber mouth-pieces are dear, and much care is manifested in their selection; their price varies from four to five dollars to hundreds of dollars, according to the quality of the material and the richness with which it is ornamented, some being set with gold and pearl.

The costume of the Turks varies according to social position, with some exceptions. The Turkish shirt resembles that of our women, and is worn over large cotton drawers. The feet are also covered with cotton.

This kind of covering for the feet is called terlyos; and it is sometimes replaced by small slippers of very fine leather, which are worn in socks attached to the shakschir, or large red trowsers. For walking, a peculiar species of slipper is used. In addition to the chemise and trowsers, the Turks wear, also, a long vest lined with cotton, called entari; and over this the famous caftan, which descends to the heels. This last garment, closed around the waist by means of a sash, is only an in-door dress; and a Turk of quality never appears in it in public. The caftan, in its turn, is also covered with the dschiouppeh (overcoat), some three or four inches shorter in length. In winter it is lined with fur, and the sleeves fall only to the elbow. Other garments with long sleeves, called benysch, cover all. In fine, this costume is as rich as it is inconvenient. The prophet prescribed white and yellow colors for dress, and prohibited red and yellow; but this commandment is not strictly observed.

The Turks, as almost all the Mohammedans, shave the head, with the exception of a small tuft on the top; and they cover it with a red woollen cap, around which they fold the turban. The Sultan, the ministers, the great dignitaries, and the judges, alone have the right of wearing the beard; the rest of the nation must rest contented with the moustache. The turban is the national head-dress of the Turks; but at the present day they add to it the fez cap. It remains, even after death, the distinctive Ottoman sign in the cemetery.

In their houses the Turks prefer comfort to elegance; but it differs widely from our own. We have need of a great quantity of furniture; while the Turk is satisfied when, with pipe in mouth, and reclining upon a divan, he can enjoy his ease. In every room there is a kind of seat against the walls, raised about two feet above the floor, and three or four feet in width, running around the apartment, which is composed of soft mattrasses, covered with cotton, cloth, or velvet, according to the means of the proprietor of the house, with high cushions for backs. It is in the luxury of these divans, and the richness of their material and color, and the magnificence of the carpets, that the Ottoman dwellings are distinguished. The Turks neither make use of chairs nor tables; the divan is a substitute for all, and frequently it serves them for a bed.

In Turkey stoves and chimneys are unknown; and people warm themselves by means of earthen or brass braziers, which are placed alongside of the divan. These *mangals*, as they are called, are generally put under a table spread with a carpet, which, falling down upon all sides, preserves the heat of the few live coals it contains. A stuffed seat with a back surrounds this table (*tandur*), at which several persons may be seated. From the commencement of cold weather, the women rarely quit their *tandur*.

The harem, or apartment of the women, in Turkey, forms a separate part of the house, and it is connected with the portion inhabited by the men by means of a gallery. This arrangement divides the house into a great number of rooms, which pleases the Turkish taste. Besides his ordinary residence, every rich or distinguished person possesses also his Kiosk, or summer pavilion, along the umbrageous shores of the Bosphorus, where he may calmly contemplate the passing fleets of vessels sailing to and fro between the Black Sea and the capital. The form of these Kiosks is either square or round, of wood, and elegantly painted both on the outside and interior, with windows closed by lattice-work. Their furniture consists of nothing but carpets and divans.

The Prophet authorized his followers to take several wives, but it would be a grave error to believe that this has led to a profligacy of morals. The Koran, on every page, inculcates chastity and decency, and the organization of the harem itself demonstrates that the commandments of their religion have entered into the morals of the Mussulmans. The women occupy a part of the house, as isolated as a cloister. The harem, in its Ottoman acceptation, is a sacred place where virtue reigns, and which is hermetically closed against all strange intrusion. The separation of the sexes is so absolute, that no servant of the house, not even an eunuch, can penetrate into the harem. The women are served only by female slaves. The nearest relatives, brothers, fathers-in-law or fathers, are only admitted in the two fêtes of Bairam, at marriages, or a circumcision. A woman is not allowed to address any one unveiled, except her near relatives, with whom marriage is prohibited. Physicians are only permitted to visit a female patient in the presence of the husband or a slave, and they cannot feel the pulse unless the arm is covered with muslin.

With such laws, it is difficult for women to deviate from the path of honor and virtue. Should they be going to the bath, or on a visit to a relative, or shopping, they must be accompanied by other women, as well as by their slaves. Women of distinction are rarely seen in the streets, for it is considered *mauvais ton* to leave the house, except from necessity. Gadding about in flaunting attire for pastime, or the indulgence of an idle vanity, is considered a vulgar practice, befitting only the wives and daughters of the ghiaours. It is for this reason that only women of low extraction are generally seen in the streets, and even these are veiled, very reserved in their behavior, and rarely speak to any one.

The most important, and almost the only domestic fêtes, are marriages. The law permits the Turks to unite themselves with a woman in three ways: the first, by marriage, the second by making a sort of engagement with her, and the third by purchase. A marriage can only be celebrated on Friday evening, which corresponds to our Sunday. The second mode, called *capin*, requires no other formality than that of going before a cadi, and in making an engagement to keep and maintain the woman for a certain fixed period of time. The father of the man, or two other relatives, must confirm it. He obliges himself, in case children should be born from such a union, to provide for their support, and to pay a certain sum to the woman, if he should send her away before the expiration of the contract. The children of such a connexion have equal rights with the others, and the father must keep them under all circumstances. But this kind of marriage is very rare. The third mode is the purchase of a slave.* The children from this union are free, and have a right to inherit from the father.

* Slaves are generally carefully educated, for their value depends not only on their physical beauty, but upon the talents they possess. The young girls learn to dance, sing, play on an instrument, and to embroider. The young boys are reared with yet greater care, and the superior ones among them are sold at high prices. Some of them, purchased for the Seraglio, acquire the favor of the Sultan, and may become great personages; for the prejudice which, among the Greeks and Romans, stamped the slave with an indelible stigma, is entirely unknown to the Mahommedans. The Mussulman women treat their slaves as sisters and daughters, and the

Another domestic *fête*, is that which takes place on a circumcision. This operation is not obligatory, for if it has been neglected in youth, a certificate of the physician that it would be dangerous, is a sufficient reason for dispensing with it. It is rarely omitted, however. The uncircumcised, *akhalf*, enjoy but little consideration, and they cannot testify as witnesses before a judge. Children

---

Oriental monarchs frequently entrust to these young captives, whom they have sometimes even admitted to the honor of their alliance, the highest dignities of the empire. In our days, the Grand Vizir, Khosrew, and Halil Pacha, son-in-law of Sultan Mahmoud, are examples of fortune, but little in accordance with European notions, and particularly with those prevalent in the new world.

Among the slaves whose career has been the most singular, history yet preserves the remembrance of the Countess Potocka. This young and beautiful slave, exposed for sale at the bazaar of Constantinople, was bought, about the close of the 18th century, by a French nobleman, the Marquis de V——, who, shortly afterwards, quitted the Levant to return to France with his precious treasure. Upon arriving at Kaminiek, Mde V—— was received with the highest regards by the Count de Witt, a Hollander in the service of Russia, and governor of the place. The Count was hardly thirty years of age; he was a lieutenant-general, stood high in the favor of Catharine II., and to these advantages united a prepossessing exterior. He was so struck by the beauty of the young slave, that he fell desperately in love, and offered to marry her. She accepted him, and abandoned her first master. Two years after his marriage, Count Witt obtained a *congé*, and visited all the courts of Europe. Everywhere, the beauty of his wife excited the liveliest admiration. At Hamburg, Count Felix Potocki, commander-in-chief, and grand master of the artillery of the republic of Poland, could not resist the charms of the beautiful Oriental, and to gratify his passion, he obliged the general to a divorce. Thus the young girl, sold at the bazaar of Constantinople, became by turns the slave of a French nobleman, the wife of a general, and finally the companion of one of the most illustrious men of Poland!

are generally circumcised in the seventh year, and in the paternal house, in the presence of the relatives, the grandmother and father, and of the Imam of the nearest mosque. The operators are called Sunnet Dschys; they all employ a razor. During the eight or ten days which follow this mutilation, the relatives exert themselves to amuse the newly-circumcised, and they carry him about, here and there, as if in triumph. They decorate his garments, his turban in particular, with gilt or silver bands, as well as with rich tufts of feathers. It is also customary to kill a lamb or a kid on such an occasion, and to distribute alms. The Sultans, in these ceremonies, display all the splendor and magnificence of the throne.

The use of the bath is so general among Mussulmans, that bath-houses are to be found in the smallest towns of the empire. That of Mustapha Pasha, at Constantinople, is one of the most elegant. It is built of cut stone, and is of the form of a parallelogram. The pavement is of different marbles; in the centre is a large reservoir filled with water, and the dome is sustained by richly carved columns. In entering the first hall of the establishment, the hammandji (master of the bath,) conducts the new comer to the divan assigned to him. In the centre of the hall is a fountain, and all around the wall runs a divan; it is here that the bather undresses. The attendant presents you with a napkin, with which you envelope the waist; then another is bound around the head. In leaving the divan, high-heeled leather slippers are put on, with which you shuffle into the second chamber. Here the temperature is more elevated, and you remain within it until the perspiration pours off the body. Then commence the important operations.

You are conducted into a third apartment, lighted by circular glass inserted in the dome. On entering, you perceive that the heat is much greater than in the preceding chamber. While the attendants are occupied with other bathers, you smoke a pipe and drink a cup of coffee.

Your turn is come, for one of the attendants of the bath stands ready to shampoo you. He first examines with the hand if the skin is in a proper condition. If he deems the moment favorable, he invites you to stretch yourself at full length upon a slab of white marble in the middle of the hall, some three feet above the floor, and which is heated by an oven beneath. You lay on your face on this table, but not without precaution; for there is some risk in burning the skin from contact with the hotter parts of the marble. Before beginning, the attendant makes a final experiment; he strikes you with a rather severe blow on the shoulder or thigh; and if the noise produced by the compressed air makes the vaulted roof resound, he hesitates no longer.

The sensations produced by shampooing are far from agreeable. This pressure of the muscles, and manipulation of the flesh and members, is painful. The *coup de grace* is particularly formidable; this last manœuvre consists in cracking the joints by strongly pressing the knee in the midst of the arms folded on the breast. The shampooing usually lasts about twenty minutes. This torture finished, you repose an instant, then enter another chamber, where softer impressions await you. A boy pours warm water upon your head in profusion, and then vigorously rubs the body with a coarse hair glove. The *douches* and the friction are repeated until the skin is perfectly cleansed, and the blood may be seen circulating through the transparent veins.

You then pass into another hall, where you are washed from head to foot with water perfumed with Candia soap. After being sponged with a handful of tow, a basin of the same saponaceous water is placed before you, in which you wash yourself free from all remaining impurities.

The operation is now finished, and the attendant dries your head and limbs, envelopes them in clean linen, and leads you to the first chamber on entering. You recline upon a divan, with the head raised upon cushions, to prevent congestion of the brain. By degrees the agitation caused by the heat, the shampooing, and the frictions, gives way to a calm quietude, which invites to sleep. The attendant then replaces the moist linen, with which the body is enveloped with other linen, which effectually dries the whole surface. A pipe and cup of coffee are presented, as in the third chamber. At last, when you feel sufficiently cool to go into the air without danger, you dress and call the boy, who presents a mirror, upon which you deposit the price of the bath.

The Turkish ladies are very fond of frequenting the baths. Friday is the day fixed for the gratification of this religious duty and the distractions which accompany it. They pass almost all the day in its pleasures, and frequently eat their meals there. The entrance of the women's baths is rigidly interdicted to the men, and they are conducted with perfect order and decency.

The moderate price that is asked for a bath permits the poor as well as the rich to enjoy it. It is quite common for the *hammandjis* (the proprietors of these establishments,) to ask nothing of those whose exterior denotes their destitution; and it is a sort of alms, in their opinion, which is equivalent to the glass of water of the Gospel.

FIFTH PART.

GEOGRAPHICAL SKETCH OF TURKEY—OF ITS PRINCIPAL TOWNS, FORTRESSES, AND OTHER PLACES CONNECTED WITH ITS MILITARY HISTORY.

The Turkish empire, the territorial possessions of which extend over a large portion of Europe, Asia, and Africa, covers a surface of about 21,000 square leagues, and comprises a total population of 35,000,000, distributed as follows: —

Turkey in Europe.	Thrace	1,800,000	
	Bulgaria	3,000,000	
	Moldavia	1,400,000	
	Wallachia	2,600,000	
	Bosnia and Herzovingia	1,000,000	
	Roumelia	2,700,000	
	Albania	1,200,000	
	Servia	1,000,000	
	Islands	700,000	
			15,500,000
Turkey in Asia.	Asia Minor	10,000,000	
	Syria, Mesopotamia, and Kurdistan	4,500,000	
	Arabia, Mecca, Medina, and Ethiopia	900,000	
			16,200,000
	Egypt	2,000.000	
	Tripoli, Fez, Tunis	1,800,000	
			3,800,000
	Total		35,500,000

The classification of this population, which is reduced to 26,700,000, if the tributary provinces be excluded, is as follows, distributed according to races: —

Races.	In Europe.	In Asia.	In Africa.	Total.
Ottomans	2,150,000	10,800,000	———	12,950,000
Sclavonians	6,200,000	———	———	6,200,000
Roumeliotes....	4,000,000	———	———	4,000,000
Albanians......	1,450,000	———	———	1,450,000
Greeks.........	1,000,000	1,000,000	———	2,000,000
Armenians.....	400,000	2,000,000	———	2,400,000
Jews..........	70,000	80,000	———	150,000
Tartars........	16,000	50,000	———	66,000
Arabs*........	———	900,000	3,800,000	4,700,000
Syrians and Chaldeans	———	250,000	———	250,000
Druses.........	———	30,000	———	30,000
Kurds..........	———	1,000,000	———	1,000,000
Turkomans.....	———	90,000	———	90,000
Gipsies	214,000	———	———	214,000
	15,500,000	16,200,000	3,800,000	35,500,000

Arranged according to religions, it gives the following results: —

Religions.	In Europe.	In Asia.	In Africa.	Total.
Mussulmans......	4,600,000	12,650,000	3,800,000	21,050,000
Greeks†	10,000,000	3,000,000		13,000,000
Catholics‡	660,000	280,000		940,000
Jews............	90,000	80,000		170,000
Different sects...				340,000
	15,350,000	16,010,000	3,800,000	35,500,000

* Including the African population, the basis of which is Arabic.

† With the Armenians.

‡ Under this category are included all the Oriental churches recognising the authority of the Holy See, although the forms of worship vary; they are: 1. The Latins or Catholics who use the Roman Liturgy. They have a Patriarch resident at Jerusalem since 1847, and besides the Bosnians and Albanian Catholics, they consist of Greeks, Armenians, Alepponians, Bulgarians, Croats, &c., to the number of 680,000. 2. The United Greeks, or Melchites, who have a Patriarch resident at Damascus, and eight suffragan sees,

The principal river of Turkey is the Danube, which enters the empire at Belgrade, and empties by five different mouths into the Black Sea, where it forms a marshy delta (bogasi). Its chief tributaries on the right are the Save, 590 miles long, which joins it at Belgrade, the Morava, the Timok, the Isker; on the left, the Czerna, the Schill, the Aluta, the Ardsisch, the Jalonitza, the Sereth, and the Pruth. The other rivers are the Maritza, which empties into the Archipelago, after traversing Roumelia, and passing by Philippopolis and Adrianople; the Koralou, the Baodar, the Indische-Karafou, the Salambria, and the Elkeda, which also enter the Archipelago. In the Ionian Sea fall the Rolia, the Æspropotamos, the Arta, and the Kalamos; in the Mediterranean, the Iris; and in the Adriatic, the Vojussa, the Ergent, the Toti, the Mati, the Drin, the Bojane, and the Narenta. The principal fortresses are Belgrade, Widdin, Silistria, Roustschouck, Shumla, Varna, in Bulgaria, Scutari, in Albania, Zwornick, Behacz, and Banjalouka in Bosnia, Bassora, Trebisond, Jean d'Acre, Alexandria, and some other less important defences, such as the citadels of Smyrna, Bagdad, Tripoli, and Cairo. The fortresses which protect the Straits of the Dardanelles and Bosphorus, and the Balkan range of mountains, the real bastions of the empire, also deserve mention.

The principal mountain ranges of Turkey are those of

25,000. 3. The Armenians united, whose Patriarch, residing at Bezoumme in the Lebanon range, has under him seven Archbishops *in paribus*, and for suffragans, the bishops of Aleppo, Mardin, and Amasia Tekar, 75,000. 4. The United Syrians and Chaldeans, with Patriarchs at Mossoul and Aleppo, and fifteen suffragans, 20,000. 5. The Maronites, with their Patriarch at Cannobin, in the Lebanon, and seven suffragan bishops, 140,000. Total, 940,000.

the Pindus, dividing Thessaly and Greece, the Lebanon running through the heart of Syria and Palestine, and the great and little Balkan. This celebrated range is less remarkable for its height, the loftiest summits not being above 7000 feet, than for its precipitous sides, thickly overgrown foreground, and the narrowness of its passes. That part which lies nearest to the Black Sea, contains seven passes; the most important is that into which converge all the roads from Bessarabia and the Dobrutscha, and Rassova, Silistria, &c., which unite at Shumla. This defile is defended by the impregnable Shumla. The pass of the iron door, Demir-Kapu, unites all the routes which, starting from the Danubian strongholds of Turtukay, and running to Sistova, lead to Constantinople.

The Dobrutscha, a marshy and pestilential tract lying between the Danube and the Black Sea, and over which the Danube is once supposed to have flowed, is the high road for an army directing its course to Constantinople, or of one advancing from the south against Bessarabia and Podolia. This peninsula is bounded on the south by the wall of Trajan, and includes the fortified towns of Toultscha, Matschin, Hirsovia, and Kustendji. In 1828–9, the Russians passed the Balkan from the Dobrutscha, having first obtained possession of Varna, on the Black Sea. For the sixth time, they have again taken up their position in this district, for the purpose of reaching Adrianople by the mountain route; but the inability to take Varna, in consequence of its great strength, and protection by the allied fleets, will probably defeat their plans of penetrating to the Turkish capital.

The Ottoman empire is divided into *Eyalets*, or general governments, whose administrators are called *Vali* (viceroy), or mutecharif (governor-general). The Eyalets are subdivided into provinces (*Livas*), at the head of which are the kainakams (lieutenant-governors), or mohassils (prefects); the Livas are divided into cazas (districts), and the cazas into Nahijes (communes).

Turkey in Europe is composed of 15 Eyalets, 42 Livas, and 376 Cazas. The Eyalets are: 1, Edirne (Thrace); 2, Silistria (Bulgaria); 3, Boydhan (Moldavia); 4, Eflak (Wallachia); 5, Widdin (Bulgaria); 6, Nissa (Bulgaria); 7, Uskup (Eastern Albania); 8, Syrp (Servia); 9, the fortress of Belgrade; 10, Bosna (Bosnia and Croatia); 11, Roumili (Albania and Macedonia); 12, Yania (Epirus); 13, Selanik (Macedonia and Thessaly); 14, Djizair (Archipelago); 15, Cryt (Crete), with governors-general at: 1, Adrianople; 2, Silistria; 3, Jassy; 4, Bucharest; 5, Widdin; 6, Nissa; 7, Uskup; 8, Belgrade; 9, Serajevo; 10, Monastir; 11, Janina; 12, Salonica; 13, Rhodes; and 14, Candia.

Turkey in Asia is divided into 18 *Eyalets*, 83 *Livas*, and 885 *Cazas*. The Eyalets are: 1, Kastamouni (Paphlagonia); 2, Khoudavenguiar (Bithynia); 3, Aydin (Lydia); 4, Caraman (Phrygia and Pamphylia); 5, Adana (Cilicia); 6, Bozoq (Cappadocia); 7, Sivas (Cappadocia); 8, Tarabezoun (Pontus and Colchis); 9, Erzeroum (Armenia); 10, Moussoul (Assyria); 11, Kurdistan; 12, Kharberout (Sophene and Comagene); 13, Halep (Syria and Orsoene); 14, Saida (Phenicia and Palestine); 15, Cham (Syria); 16, Bagdad; 17, Habesch (Arabia and Ethiopia); and 18, Armin-Nabevi, with governors-general at: 1, Kastamouni; 2, Brusa; 3, Smyrna; 4, Konia; 5, Adana; 6, Angora; 7, Sivas; 8, Trebizond; 9, Erzeroum; 10, Moussoul; 11, Diarbekir; 12, Charpout; 13, Aleppo; 14, Beyrout; 15, Damascus; 16, Bagdad; 17, Djedda; and 18, Medina.

Turkey in Africa is divided into 3 *Eyalets*, 17 *Livas*, 86 *Cazas*. The Eyalets are: 1, Missr (Egypt); 2, Tarablousi-Gharde (Tripoli in Africa); 3, Tunis, with governor at Cairo; 2, Tripoli; and 3, Tunis.

I. TERRITORIAL POSSESSIONS OF THE TURKISH EMPIRE IN EUROPE.

CONSTANTINOPLE, called *Istamboul* by the Turks; capital of the empire, with the suburbs of Pera and Galata, and Scutari (the latter on the opposite Asiatic shore, but forming an integral part of the metropolis), numbers 750,000 inhabitants, thus divided: 450,000 Ottomans, 180,000 Greeks, 50,000 Jews, 40,000 Franks (Christians), and about 30,000 land and naval troops. It is situated between the Black Sea and the Sea of Marmora, at the entrance of the Bosphorus, and upon the channel which separates Europe from Asia, and whose depth and sheltered position form one of the finest harbors in the world; the residence of the Sultan, the Mufti, the ministers, and all the grandees of the empire. The Christian and Israelitish religions are all represented there by their respective patriarchs and high priests. It contains 346 mosques, 518 medreces, or superior schools, 300 public baths, more than 1200 primary schools, and 35 public libraries, each containing from one to two thousand volumes, and rare collections of precious manuscripts. From its magnificent position on the borders of Europe and Asia, midway between the remote East and the Christian states of the world, its commercial advantages, its superiority as a dominating point over the Black Sea and the Levant, and the beauty of its environs, it is one of the most remarkable cities on the globe.

Cities in Roumelia.

ADRIANOPLE, in Turkish Edrene, upon the banks of the Tundscha; second capital of the empire, with 150,000 inhabitants, 134 m. N. W. of Constantinople, on one of the richest plains in the world.

TSCHIRMEN, capital of a sandschack, with 8000 inhabitants.

DSCHISR-MUSTAPHA, upon the Maritsa, with 2000 inhabitants.

DEMOTIKA, 15,000 inhabitants, the residence of a Greek archbishop.

KIRKHILISSI, with 16,000 inhabitants.

BURGAS, small town on the Black Sea, very important in time of war, for its excellent harbor, 7000 inhabitants.

In the interior of the Empire are:

PHILIPPOPOLIS, large town with 80,000 inhabitants, seat of a Greek archbishopric. The most thriving of the manufacturing towns of Turkey, in silk, woollen, and cotton stuffs.

TATAR-BASARDSCHIK, upon the grand route from Belgrade to Constantinople, 10,000 inhabitants.

ESKI-SAGRA, at the foot of the Balkan, 20,000 inhabitants.

KASANLAK, in the gorges of the Balkan, 10,000 inhabitants.

SELIMNIA, near the iron gate of the Balkan, 20,000 inhabitants. One of the largest fairs of the empire is held here; a manufactory of arms.

URUNDSCHOWA, important commercial town, famous for its large fairs.

KAWALA, upon the coast of the Archipelago, with a port and 3000 inhabitants.

ENOS, the port of Adrianople, near the mouth of the Maritza, 36 m. N.W. of Gallipoli, at the head of the Archipelago.

GALLIPOLI, upon a peninsula of the same name, in the sea of Marmora, with a good harbor at the entrance of the Dardanelles, 17,000 inhabitants. Large manufactures of morocco, with an extensive commerce, and vast magazines for the provisioning of the Ottoman fleet; first town taken by the Turks in Europe.

KILID-BAHR, the most important fortification of the Dardanelles, mounting 155 cannon, opposite the castle of Asia.

SULTANI-CALESSI, on the Dardanelles, Asiatic castle, 196 cannon, 18 of which are of the largest calibre.

BOVALLI-CALESSI, site of the ancient Sestos, a castle of the Dardanelles, with 50 cannon. All the batteries together on the European shore number 336 guns, 4 of which are mortars; those on the shore of Asia contain 486 cannon and 4 mortars. In all the fortresses on the Dardanelles there are 822 cannon and 8 mortars.

RODOSTO, a flourishing commercial town, constantly increasing.

Principal towns of Macedonia.

SALONICA, (ancient Thessalonica,) on the gulf of the same name, the most important place of commerce in European Turkey, after Constantinople. 60,000 inhabitants, two-thirds of whom are Turks, the rest Jews, Franks, and Greeks. Exports raw cotton, tobacco, wool, silk, wheat, linseed, hempseed, &c.; in 1837, amounting in value to nearly $1,000,000.

SEDES, village with mineral springs and baths.

JENIDSCHE-VARDAR, 6000 inhabitants.

KARAFERIA, manufacturing town, 20,000 inhabitants.

VODINA, (anc. Edessa.)

SERES, not far from Takino, 30,000 inhabitants: near to it is

ATHOS, with 16 cloisters, and more than 300 chapels, cells, and grottoes, inhabited by 4000 monks.

KASTORIA, USKUP, KOPROLO (with a stone bridge over the Vardar); STROMZA, PETROVICH (with large tobacco plantations), KUSTENDIL, KARATOVA, and BITOGLIA.

The most important towns of Thessaly are:

LARISSA, upon the banks of the Solambria; seat of a Greek archbishopric. 30,000 inhabitants. Here all the routes of Thessaly converge. In its vicinity is

TRIKALA, with a fort; 12,000 inhabitants. Near the defile of Agrafa.

TURNAVOS, AMBELAKIA, on the slopes of Mt. Ossa, once celebrated for spinning and dyeing cotton yarn.

The principal towns of Bulgaria are:

SHUMLA, one of the strongest positions of Europe, and one of the advanced ramparts of the empire; on the northern side of the Balkan, 290 m. N.N.W. from Constantinople, on one of the main roads to which it lies. The Russians failed in all their attacks upon this impregnable fortress in 1774, 1810, and 1828. Its tinmen and braziers are the best in Turkey, and carry on active trade with the capital; population 30,000.

MADARA, large village, inhabited by 2000 Mahommedan women who live in common.

RASGRADE, small town.

ROUSTSCHOUK, a fortified town on the Danube, with 33,000 inhabitants, composed of Armenians, Greeks, Turks, and Jews; large manufactures and flourishing commerce.

SILISTRIA, strongly fortified on the Danube, 20,000 population. Defended in 1829 for two months by 1200 Turks against 50,000 Russians.

BOSARDSCHICK, important town for its position on the Danube.

VARNA, one of the best ports of the Black Sea, the ancient Odessus, 47 m. E. Shumla, surrounded by fortifications of immense strength, the mart of an extensive and fertile region. It produces excellent wines and fruits, and carries on a large trade in leather, tallow, wax, honey, building timber, &c. It has an advantage over its rival, Odessa, in the fact that its harbor does not freeze.

KARNABAD and PARAVADI, upon the military route of the Balkan.

DEMIR-CAPU, *iron gate*, celebrated passage of the Balkan from Selimnia in Roumelia, to Stareka in Bulgaria.

SOPHIA, between the Isker and Nissava, population 50,000.

WIDDIN, strong fortress on the Danube, population 25,000.

SISTOVA, beautifully situated on the Danube, and famous for its cotton and leather manufactures.

RASSOVA and HIRSOVA, strong citadels.

NICOPOLIS, on the Danube, which is here 6 miles broad. 10,000 population.

MATSCHIN, ISAKCHI, and TULCHA, fortified towns for the defence of the right bank of the Danube, and which have acquired great importance since the Turks have been forced to change their lines of defence from Braila, Giurgewo, and Turna, Tultscha commands the forks of the Danube, and at Isakschi there is a ferry, over which is the general route from lower Bulgaria to Wallachia.

BABA-DAGH, 10,000 inhabitants, and TURNAVE, 9000 population, are important military points.

In Albania are:

JOANINNA, upon a lake, the former capital of the blood-thirsty Ali Pasha; 18,000 population. In the neighborhood are:

MEZZOVO, 7000 population; KONITZA, PREMITI, CLISIURA, celebrated citadels; DELVINO, with a strong fort, and 8000 population; SULI, memorable for the valor of its inhabitants, and PARAMITHIA.

AGIROCASTRO, 9000 population, OCHRIDA, DUKAGIN, and PERSERENDI, 4000 inhabitants.

ALESSUS, at the mouth of the Drin, and CROYA, 6000 population.

SCUTARI, large fortified town, 20,000 population, flourishing commerce, and formerly celebrated by the brilliant court of Mustapha.

DULCIGNIO, in the Adriatic, 2500 population. ANTIVARI, seat of a Greek metropolitan, a mile from the roadstead of that name.

ARTA (anc. Ambracia), 6000 population; SALAGORE, PRERESA, with a harbor. PARGA, on the Adriatic, BUTRINTO, formerly a Venetian fortress; JAKOVA, 20,000 population; DURAZZO (anc. Dyrrachium), 5000 population, commercial trade.

Principal towns of Bosnia:

BOSNA-SERAI, large town on the Migliazza, with walls and ramparts, small forts, and 70,000 population; large manufactures of arms, iron, copper, wool, cotton; central point of Bosnian commerce.

TRAVNICK, with a citadel, 8000 population. Seat of the Grand Vizir of this *Eyalet*, to whom the Porte gives the honorary title of Vizir of Hungary.

VADROUK and MAGLAI, small towns on the Bosnia, with good citadels.

ZWORNICK, one of the three fortresses of Bosnia; 14,000 population.

MOSTAR, upon the Narenta, 9000 population; celebrated for its stone bridge, of which one arch has a span of 300 feet.

BIHACZ, one of the great fortresses of Bosnia. NOVI, small town, with citadel and important trade.

JAICZA, small town, with strong castle.

BANJALUKA, large town of the Sandschack of the same name; 15,000 population. One of the three great fortresses of Bosnia.

DESBIR, small fortified town.

LIVNO, town upon the great route of Austrian Dalmatia; flourishing commerce, 4000 population.

TREBINJE, strong town, 10,000 population.

Principal towns of the island of Candia:

CANDIA (Kirid in Turkish), capital of the island. Good citadel, and about 15,000 population; remarkable for its remains of the Venetian domination, with a good harbor, but shallow.

STANDIA, small island near Candia, with some good harbors.

RETYMO, town of Candia, with a harbor and port; 6000 population.

CANEA, most frequented port of the island; 12,000 population.

SFAKIA, chief town of the Sfakists of the island.

SPINALONGA, small fortress, upon the north side of the island;

good harbor, and 2000 population. The island of Candia is 110 miles from the coast of Asia Minor, is about 160 miles long, and 20 miles broad. Total population 160,000, of whom 100,000 are native Greeks, 40,000 Turks, remainder Jews, Franks, &c. In ancient times supposed to have contained 1,200,000 inhabitants, and under the Venetians, 600,000; highly rich and fertile soil, producing cotton, tobacco, wheat, barley, oats, oil, figs, wine, oranges, lemons, linseed, honey, &c. Its numerous mountains are covered with luxuriant forests of oak, chestnut, walnut, pine, cypress, &c., and haunted by wild boar, wild goat, &c. Climate healthy, and but few endemic diseases. It is governed by a pasha, who is either an European or Asiatic Turk.

Five other of the principal islands of the Archipelago, belonging to Turkey, merit notice: —

Cyprus, 300 m. east of Candia, is 132 m. long, and 35 m. broad. Population, 100,000; one of the most fertile soils in the world, producing, in abundance, grapes, lemons, oranges, figs, olives, oil, silk, &c., with extensive forests of pine, beech, and oak. Its wheat and cotton are of a superior quality; and its neglected copper mines, in ancient times, were worked with great profit; its mountains also contain gold, silver, and iron; and near Baffa, asbestos is found in large quantities. It is one of the most prolific regions of the East for the grape. Owing to misgovernment, the population, which, in ancient times, amounted to 1,000,000, has greatly declined. Possesses, however, all the elements of prosperity; abounds in good harbors. Larnica, the consular residence, on the coast, has 5000 inhabitants; restored by Egypt to Turkey in 1840, and now forms a separate *Eyalet.*

Samos, off the coast of Asia Minor, is 175 square miles in extent, and although mountainous, it is very fertile, producing a great variety of fruits, and abounding in forests of chestnuts, oak, platane trees, as well as medicinal plants, such as jalap, scammony, &c., and mines of emery, marble, iron; loadstone and ochre pits are also found. Population, 60,000, in a state of demi-independence; inhabitants turbulent enemies of the Ottoman yoke.

Rhodes, ten miles from coast of Asia Minor, 36 m. long, 14 m. broad. Population, 50,000; produces corn, wine, oil, cotton, fruit, wax, honey. Capital town, Rhodes; population, 8000, with the houses and fortifications of the Knights of St. John yet standing.

Scio, a magnificent island, separated from Asia by a strait eight miles wide, contains 392 square miles; climate very healthy. Famous for its luxuriant production of silk, cotton, oranges, lemons, figs, wine, mastic, &c., and its beautiful women. Chief city, Scio, on the east side, with a population of 15,000. The whole population of the island previous to the massacre of 1822, 100,000, now about 40,000. It is the paradise of the Archipelago.

Mytilene (ancient Lesbos), on the northern edge of the Gulf of Smyrna, 50,000 inhabitants; one of the best cultivated islands, and in a state of high prosperity; raises excellent wine, olives, grain, figs, and other fruits. Chief town, Castro; 10,000 population; 137 miles in circumference; 260 square miles in extent.

II. TERRITORIAL POSSESSIONS OF TURKEY IN ASIA.

The frontiers of this natal country, as it were, of the Ottomans are: to the north, the Dardanelles, the sea of Marmora, the Bosphorus, the Black Sea, and Russia in Asia; to the east, Russia in Asia, and the kingdom of Persia; to the south, Arabia; to the west, the Mediterranean and the Archipelago. Turkey in Asia is divided into eighteen *Eyalets*, or general governments. The principal points (which we can alone mention) are:

Kutahije, population 50,000; seat of the Beglerberg of Anatolia, and of a molla.

Brusa, at the foot of Mount Olympus, one of the most prosperous towns of the empire; population 100,000. The capital of the empire, down to the taking of Adrianople. The seat of a molla of the first class, of a pasha, a Greek metropolitan, and an Arminian archbishop. Celebrated for the fertility of its adjacent plains, and its superior manufactures of silk and cotton fabrics, carpets, and velvets, its khans and colleges, its hot baths, and the charming beauty of its situation.

MUDANIA, on the sea of Marmora, with a harbor, by means of which it is put in communication with Constantinople and Europe. It is the port of Brusa.

SMYRNA, upon the gulf of that name. Large and beautiful town, with one of the most extensive bazaars of the East; principal seat of Asiatic commerce with Europe. Exports raisins, figs, opium, Turkey carpets, rhubarb, raw silk, cotton, &c. 150,000 population; one half Turks, the residue Franks, and a representation of all the nations of the East.

VOURLA, small town on the gulf of Smyrna (anc. Clazemene). Seat of the Greek archbishop of Ephesus, and one of the best naval harbors of the empire.

NICODEMIA, one of the largest cities of the Roman empire; as the capital of which it was selected by Dioclesian; at the extremity of a gulf five miles wide, and thirteen miles deep, on the sea of Marmora; 5500 houses, but only 30,000 population. Constantine the Great died here.

In this part of Anadolia, to the south and opposite to the island of Tenedos, is the bay of Besika, near the entrance of the Dardanelles from the Archipelago, the anchorage-ground of the allied fleets.

DEMONESI, or Princes' Islands, a group of islets in the Sea of Marmora, within sight of Constantinople, at the entrance of the Bosphorus.

MARMORA, the largest island of the sea of that name. Celebrated for its marble quarries.

BODROUN, ancient Halicarnassus. Port and dock-yards for construction of Turkish vessels of war.

MARMORIZZA, small island to the south, containing one of the finest harbors in the Mediterranean.

TARSOUS, formerly the most beautiful, richest, and most powerful city of Cilicia; flourishing commerce; population 30,000.

PAYAS, small town on the Gulf of Alexandretta.

MERASCH, in the interior of the country, capital of the government of the same name.

KONIEH, formerly residence of the Sultans of Roumelia, and at present seat of a Greek Metropolitan and a Pasha. Important for its carpet and morocco manufactures; population 30,000.

TOKAT, large town, with an European aspect. Seat of an Armenian archbishopric. Famous as a point of gathering for caravans, for its copper foundries, dye-works, and Turkey leather manufactories; population 90,000.

TREBISOND, on the Black Sea, with a magnificent roadstead and two harbors. The port of European trade with India, Persia, &c., and the emporium of all the countries to the S. E. of the Black Sea. Veins of copper and lead in the neighboring mountains. Manufactures of arms and other articles; a flourishing place, and of great prospective importance; population 50,000. An Austrian and Turkish line of steamers run regularly between this city and Constantinople.

BATOUN, small port on the Black Sea, near Trebisond and the Russian frontier, latterly known as the base of the Turkish operations in their attack on Fort Nikolajew; population 6000.

ERZEROUM, near the north shore of the Euphrates, important city of Turkish Armenia, on an elevated plain; 134 m. S. E. of Trebisond — highly flourishing trade — on the high road between Asia Minor, Georgia, and Persia; manufactures of arms and the best sabres of the empire — the Ottoman rampart against Russia and Persia.

DIARBEKIR, upon the right bank of the Tigris, large and beautiful town; seat of a Chaldean patriarch, of a Catholic bishop, and a Jacobite patriarch. Manufactures and commerce; population 55,000.

MOSUL, on the Tigris, 193 m. N. N. W. Bagdad, population 50,000; near the site of the ancient Nineveh, very healthy climate, important manufactures of *muslins*.

BAGDAD, on the Tigris, 200 miles from its junction with the Euphrates, built on both banks of the river, here about 650 feet wide, and connected by a bridge of boats. Maintains an active trade with Asia Minor, Syria, and Europe, in the distribution by caravans of goods from India, imported at Bussorah, and thence boated up the Tigris. Merchants from all parts of the East are to be met with in its thronged bazaars. Once the residence of the caliphs, and the principal seat of Oriental learning, until it was destroyed by Genghis Khan.

BUSSORAH, on the S. W. bank of the Euphrates, 70 miles from its mouth, and 45 miles below its junction with the Tigris, and 270 S. E. of Bagdad. Grand emporium of the Turkish empire for the produce of the East Indies; accessible for vessels of 500 tons burden. 60,000 population.

ALEPPO, formerly the first city after Constantinople and Cairo, and at present containing 140,000 inhabitants; surrounded by gardens and vineyards; still a place of considerable trade. Has been overthrown on several occasions by violent earthquakes.

TRIPOLI, the best built town of all Syria, with a good harbor on the Mediterranean, and a large commerce; excellent tobacco raised in its vicinity. "Tripoli," says McCulloch, "was taken by the Crusaders in 1108. It had previously been one of the most flourishing seats of Oriental literature, and possessed a very large collection of Persian and Arabic works. It is said that 100 copyists were constantly kept employed copying manuscripts, and that the princes of Tripoli were in the habit of sending messengers into foreign countries to discover and purchase rare and valuable works. Unfortunately, however, this extensive and precious collection, amounting, it is said, to 100,000 volumes, was destroyed by the Crusaders, who displayed on this occasion the same fanatical zeal of which they have accused, though we believe unjustly, the Arabs in the case of the Alexandrian library. A priest in the suite of Count Bertrand de St. Giles, having visited an apartment of the library in which were a number of duplicate copies of the Koran, reported that it contained none but the impious works of Mohammed, and that, consequently, it should be destroyed! And, as a matter of course, it was forthwith set on fire!

ST. JEAN D'ACRE, strong town on the sea-coast; formerly a celebrated port, but now filled with obstructions; surrounded by fortifications of great strength; sustained many memorable sieges during the crusades, and remained in the hands of the Christians for 100 years; the Saracens took it in 1291. It is at the entrance of the valley that leads to Nazareth and the heart of Palestine. 20,000 population.

JERUSALEM, the most celebrated city of the world — the cradle of Christianity and Judaism, and the second sanctuary of Mahommedanism. Beyond its sacred Christian sites, it contains one of the most elegant mosques in the Turkish dominions, that of Omar, built on the foundations of the temple of Soliman; within its precincts is the holy stone, *Hadjr el Sakhara*, with an impress of the foot of the Prophet, when he was translated to heaven. Chiefly dependent for existence as a place of resort for Christian, Hebrew, and Mahommedan pilgrims, and in its trade of holy *souvenirs*. Population about 12,000, of whom 7000 are Turks.

DAMASCUS, one of the most ancient cities of the world. 50,000 pilgrims from Turkey in Europe and Asia, Persia, and Turkestan, annually visit it; population 140,000. The Turks of this city live in great magnificence, and the bazaars, khans, and hospitals, are among the most famous in the East; place of great commerce, and a grand rendezvous of caravans for Mecca, Bagdad, Aleppo, &c. Situated in one of the most fertile and beautiful plains of the world, covered with all kinds of fruit and grains; one of the most fanatical cities of Mahommedanism.

BEYROUT, the port of Damascus on the Mediterranean, and chief town of export of Syria, on the edge of an extensive plain covered with mulberry and fig plantations; population 13,000.

III. TRIBUTARY COUNTRIES OF TURKEY IN EUROPE AND AFRICA: MOLDAVIA, WALLACHIA, SERVIA, EGYPT, TRIPOLI, AND TUNIS.

Each of the tributary countries of the Porte possesses a peculiar government under the protectorate of the Sultan.

In Servia, the prince, or Hospodar, in concert with a senate, and by the payment of an annual tribute of two millions of Turkish piasters (461,250 francs), exercises the domestic government of the principality. By treaty stipulations, the Turks cannot reside in Servia, Moldavia, and Wallachia; but they occupy the frontier Servian fortress of Belgrade in case of war, and the Hospodar is obliged to furnish an auxiliary force of 12,000 men. In conformity with the conditions of the treaty of Adrianople, the Sultan published a Hatti-sheriff, regulating the obligations of Servia to the Porte, leaving, however, its domestic administration entirely free. By virtue of the same decree, all the personal or other taxes, which the Sultan or Grand Vizir could increase or diminish at pleasure, have been abolished, with the exception of the yearly tribute. The incorporation with the principalities of six formerly independent districts, Timok, Carmala, Drina, Prahin, Kruschowatz, and Starrovolsk, was also determined by the treaty.

The princes (Waiwodes, Hospodars,) of Moldavia and Wallachia are under the sovereignty of the Porte, and the protectorate of Russia; but they are appointed by the Sultan. Their armed force, at present, amounts to 7000 regular troops, and 50,000 militia; they send no representatives to foreign nations, and have no relations with them. The hospodars are appointed by the Sultan for life, and are selected from among the boyards of the first class, according to the treaty of 1829. Egypt, Tripoli, and Tunis—the first recognised as a vice-royalty, inheritable in the family of Mehemet Ali — are likewise tributary countries to the Porte.

Montenegro, a small mountainous country between Albania and Dalmatia, is altogether independent of the Porte. In an extent of about seventy square miles, it contains 130,000 inhabitants, of the Greek confession, of whom 20,000 are accustomed to the use of arms. Its constitution is almost republican, and its chief is called Wladika (bishop). The translator had the pleasure of receiving a visit, in 1851, at Naples from the predecessor of the actual Wladika. He was a tall, commanding person, thoroughly educated at a German University, a tragic poet, whose compositions had been performed with considerable success on the Vienna stage, and a warm republican in political sentiment. He spoke of his people as a warlike and semi-barbarous race, fierce lovers of liberty, for which they had valiantly contended for ages against Christian and Mussulman enemies. He was a firm believer in the superiority of the Sclavonic stock, and was particularly inimical to Kossuth and the Hungarians. Upon parting with me, he expressed the hope of receiving me among his native mountains, and of making me acquainted with his martial subjects. "The only two perfectly free countries in the world," said he, as he retired, "are the United States of America and Montenegro!" The present Wladika is Daniel I. Petrovich Njegosch, and combines the dignity of prince of the church, with that of chief of the state. He resides in the capital of Montenegro, at Cettignie, the population of which is about 6000.

1. *Principality of Moldavia.*

Moldavia is situated along the right bank of the Pruth, embraces an extent of 800 square miles, and contains 1,400,000 inhabitants. For a short distance the Danube serves as its frontier to the south; the Pruth and Sereth both empty into it. The principal towns are:

JASSY, capital of the principality on the Beglui, a tributary of the Pruth, 160 miles W. N. W. of Odessa; residence of the foreign consuls; population 40,000.

ROMAN, a town, 1800 population; seat of a bishop.

GALATZ, on the Danube, centre of the commerce of the principality, with a port, and 30,000 population; strongly fortified.

DOROHOE, capital of Upper Moldavia.

BOTTUSCHANI, the most considerable town of Upper Moldavia, for its relations with Brody, Brunn, and all Austria.

2. *The Principality of Wallachia.*

The principal rivers of Wallachia are the Danube, which forms the frontier on the side of Turkey, and its tributaries, the Schyl, the Aluta, the Ardschisch, the

Jalomitza, and Sereth. The Hospodar is appointed for life, and can be deposed only for some one of the offences laid down in the treaty of Adrianople. He exercises the free government of the province in its domestic affairs. Wallachia, as Moldavia, has the advantage of being exempt from the maintenance of a Turkish corps of occupation. The extent of its territory is 13,500 square geographic miles, and its population amounts to 2,600,000. The most important towns are:

BUCHAREST, upon the Dambrowitza, a tributary of the Danube, 280 m. W.N.W. of Constantinople, residence of consuls and the richest boyards; great commerce; population 90,000. In its vicinity are PLOYESTI, WALENI, KIMPINA, important for their commerce.

TERGOVIST, former residence of the Hospodar.

FOKSCHANI, considerable commercial town on the frontier; and

BUSNO, 4000 population.

BRAILA, fortified, with a port on the Danube; population 18,000.

GUIRGEWO, on the Danube, opposite Roustschouck, citadel upon an island; population 16,000.

SLOBODZIN, 7000 population.

ARDSISCH, celebrated for the route which traverses it, leading to the passage of the red tower.

KRAJOWA, chief town of little Wallachia; large commerce; population 17,000.

OLTENITZA, at the junction of the Ardsisch and Danube. Here the Turks crossed in 1853, and obtained an important victory under its walls.

KALAFAT, celebrated by its heroic defence by Omar Pasha, and unsuccessful siege by the Russians in 1854.

3. *Principality of Servia.*

Servia is bounded on the north by the Danube and the Save; to the west by Bosnia; to the south by Albania and Roumelia, and to the east by Bulgaria and Wallachia.

It contains 700 square geographical miles, and 1,000,000 inhabitants. The principal towns are:

SEMENDRIA, at the confluence of the Morawa and the Danube; a considerable town, fortified, and the capital of the Principality. Population 12,000.

BELGRADE, the most important and best built town of Servia, and one of the strongest fortifications of Europe; population 25,000.

NISSA, fortified town, and seat of a Greek bishopric.

KRAGOJEWATZ, the present seat of the government.

UBICZA, point of junction of many important routes.

VALLIEVO and GLODOVA, small villages on the right bank of the Danube.

SHABACZ, strongly fortified town, population 8000.

NOVIBASAR, population 7500.

With these geographical notices upon Turkey in Europe, Asia, and Africa, we have sufficiently accomplished our aim of giving, within a limited space, an outline of the natural and military resources, and population of the Ottoman empire. The present theatre of war is transferred from the immediate borders of the Danube to the country surrounding the Black Sea. This spacious sea is no doubt destined to be the scene of an immense inland commerce at some future day. The dangers of navigation from its fogs, currents, and violent winds, will be overcome when its shores shall be provided with lighthouses, and a proper map of its soundings and physical features shall have been made.

The Venitians and the Genoese were the first modern nations who appreciated and sought to avail themselves of the position and riches of the Black Sea, in ancient times visited only by the vessels of the Grecian republics. Genoa there established its route to the East Indies, neglecting that over the isthmus of Suez. It is, perhaps, to the commercial enterprise of the Genoese in the Eastern seas, that we may ascribe a reason for the energetic obstinacy with which they defended against Mahomet II. the city of Constantinople, which, for a long period, had become in their hands a vast entrepôt of trade.

Numerous and different races occupy the shores of the Euxine. In the west are the Turks and Bulgarians; further, the Russians at Odessa, Sebastopol, &c.; to the north and north-east, the Cossacks; upon the eastern shore are the Mingrelians, Georgians, the Lazes, the Abazes, and the Circassians; to the south rove the Mussulman tribes of Asia Minor.

The products of the countries bathed by this sea are no less various. The grains, cattle, and woods of Bithynia are celebrated in the East. The environs of Sinope, the ancient capital of Paphlagonia, afford tar, hemp, ship timber, and other articles requisite for the naval service. Trebisond possesses productive copper mines. The eastern coast is also very fertile, and the demi-civilised tribes who inhabit it carry on a large commerce in furs. From Georgia and Circassia the rich Mussulmans supply their harems. Who could estimate the number of victims which the inhabitants of these two countries have sacrificed to the merciless avarice of the slave merchants of Constantinople, and the insatiable voluptuousness of the dignitaries of the Ottoman empire? From these fine populations, who inhabit the cradle-land of the human race, were furnished the Mamelouks of Egypt — that redoubtable cavalry force which, for so long a period, swayed the fortunes of the land of the Pharaohs. To the north is the Crimea, whose grains are exported to all the countries of Europe; and the mouths of the Danube bring down upon its waters the rich and varied products of the vast region drained by that great stream.

From the 15th to the close of the 18th century, the Turks excluded all other nations from entering the Euxine. After 1799, the Russians finally gained a footing upon its shores, but it was only thrown open to the world at large by the treaty of Adrianople. Its exclusive possession would be a source of incalculable wealth and power to Russia, and would enable her to realize her ambitious dreams of naval supremacy in the Mediterranean. Among the mountains of the Caucasus, and the high plains of Armenia, and in the defiles of the Balkan, within sight of its waters, the hostile camps of the contending nations are now engaged in a conflict, the issue of which is to affect the interests of the whole human family.

THE END.

APPENDIX.

I.

OFFICIAL NOTE, ADDRESSED BY THE SUBLIME PORTE TO THE AMBASSADORS OF FRANCE, ENGLAND, PRUSSIA, AND AUSTRIA.

"Although the question of the Holy Places, which formed one of the objects of the mission of his Excellency, Prince Menshikoff, ambassador extraordinary of Russia, was settled to the satisfaction of all parties, the prince has advanced certain pretensions with respect to the Greek church and its clergy, of an entirely different nature.

"The Sublime Porte holds itself bound to preserve unimpaired, now and at all times, the religious immunities, as well as the rights and privileges granted under preceding reigns, and confirmed by the reigning Sultan, to the churches, monasteries, and clergy, of the Ottoman subjects professing the Greek religion; it has also never intended to violate them in any manner, nor has it ever called in question the friendly and loyal intentions of his majesty the Emperor of Russia. But to stipulate with a foreign government by a *sened* (obligatory act), under the form of a convention, or by a note or declaration having the same force and value, rights, privileges, and immunities (were they even exclusively confined to the religion, faith, and church), in favor of a numerous community, subjects of the government, this trenches upon the independent rights of the power which engages itself, and is not to be compared with concessions made by former treaties.

"The facts, however, have been frankly laid before Prince Menshikoff; and a disposition has also been manifested to give every assurance proper to dissipate the apprehensions entertained with respect to the faith which his majesty the Emperor of all the Russias, personally professes. But, unfortunately, this has not led to an understanding between the two parties; and the Sublime Porte deeply regrets that the prince has pushed matters so far as to discontinue all further relations, and to quit his post.

"The Sublime Porte cherishes no hostile intention towards the august court of Russia; its most ardent aspiration, on the contrary, is to draw yet tighter the bonds of friendship which are so dear and precious to it, by the resumption of official relations. It hopes, then, that his majesty the Emperor, in view of his well known character for justice, will not without cause engage in hostilities; and that the firm principles of his imperial Majesty, of which the world is a witness, will not permit him to adopt a course at variance with the positive assurances which he has given to the august courts of Europe.

"But as it is a fact that the prince has broken off all relations, and quitted his post; as, in this interval, the Sublime Porte has in nowise been assured that war would not take place, whilst it sees great military preparations made by Russia on land and sea, on the frontiers of the Ottoman empire, the Sublime Porte, although it has no hostile intention, finds itself obliged, however, in common precaution, to adopt certain preparatory measures; and it has resolved from this date to take measures of defence, and it trusts that the high courts, signers of the treaty of 1841, will admit the propriety of its conduct.

"In acquitting myself, by sovereign order, of this communication, I seize, etc., etc.

(Signed) "MOUSTAFA RESCHID."

II.

MANIFESTO OF THE EMPEROR OF RUSSIA.

"By the grace of God, we, Nicholas I., Emperor and Autocrat of all the Russias, etc., etc. We make known:

"By our manifesto of the 14th of June of the present year, we made known to our faithful and well-beloved subjects, the motives which obliged us to reclaim of the Ottoman Porte inviolable guarantees in favor of the sacred rights of the orthodox church.

"We likewise announced to them that all our efforts to bring back the Porte, by means of amicable persuasion, to sentiments of equity, and to the faithful observation of treaties, had failed; and that we had, consequently, deemed it indispensable to advance our troops into the Danubian principalities. But in adopting this measure, we yet entertained the hope that the Porte would recognize its errors, and would satisfy our just reclamations.

"Our expectation has been deceived.

"In vain even did the principal powers of Europe endeavor, by their exhortations, to shake the blind obstinacy of the Ottoman government. It is by a declaration of war, by a proclamation of false accusations against Russia, that it has answered to the pacific efforts of Europe, and to our forbearance. Finally, enrolling in its ranks the revolutionists of all countries, the Porte commences hostilities on the Danube. Russia is provoked to the combat—nothing more is left to it than, reposing confidently upon God, to have recourse to arms in order to constrain the Ottoman government to respect the treaties, and to obtain a reparation for the insults with which it has replied to our most moderate demands, and to our legitimate solicitude for the defence of the orthodox faith in the East, which the people of Russia also profess; convinced that our faithful subjects will unite with us in fervent prayer to the Most High, to deign to bless our arms in his holy cause, which has always found ardent defenders in our pious ancestors.

"*In te, Domine, speravi; non confundar in aeternum.*

"Given at Toarkoe-Selo, the 20th day of the month of October, of the year one thousand eight hundred and fifty-three, and of the twenty-eighth of our reign.

(Signed) "Nicholas."

III.

DECLARATION OF WAR BY ENGLAND.

"Her Majesty, with deep regret, announces the failure of her anxious and continued efforts to preserve to her people and to Europe the blessings of peace.

"The Emperor of Russia having persisted in his unprovoked aggression upon the Sublime Porte with such a disregard of the consequences, as to refuse the just and honorable propositions presented to him by the Emperors of Austria and France, the King of Prussia, and Her Majesty; Her Majesty feels herself obliged, by the honor of her crown and a due regard for the independence of the States of Europe, to repair to the defence of an ally whose territory has been invaded, and whose independence is assailed.

"In justification of the measure she has been obliged to resort to, Her Majesty refers to the events which have transpired.

"The Emperor of Russia found some motive of complaint against the Sultan, with reference to the adjustment by him of the conflicting claims between the Greek and Latin churches, to certain of the Holy Places in Jerusalem and its vicinity. The Sultan did justice, in this particular, to the complaint of the Emperor of Russia, and the ambassador of Her Majesty in Constantinople had the satisfaction of promoting an agreement to which the Russian government made no objection.

"But while the Russian government repeatedly assured the government of Her Majesty, that the mission of Prince Menschikoff to Constantinople was exclusively directed to the settlement of the question of the Holy Places at Jerusalem, Prince Menschikoff himself pressed upon the Porte other demands of a far more serious and important character, the nature of which he, in the first instance, endeavored, as far as possible, to conceal from Her Majesty's ambassador. And these demands, thus studiously concealed, affected not the privileges of the Greek Church at Jerusalem, but the position of many millions of Turkish subjects in their relations to their sovereign the Sultan.

"These demands were rejected by the spontaneous decision of the Sublime Porte.

"Two assurances have been given to Her Majesty: one, that the mission of Prince Menschikoff only regarded the Holy Places; the other, that his mission would be of a conciliatory character.

"In both respects, Her Majesty's just expectations were disappointed.

"Demands were made which, in the opinion of the Sultan, extended to the substitution of the Emperor of Russia's authority for his own over a large portion of his subjects; and those demands were enforced by a threat; and when Her Majesty learned that, on announcing the termination of his mission, Prince Menschikoff declared that the refusal of his demands would impose upon the Imperial Government the necessity of seeking a guaranty by its own power, Her Majesty thought proper that her fleet should leave Malta, and, in co-operation with that of his Majesty the Emperor of the French, take up its station in the neighborhood of the Dardanelles.

"So long as the negotiation bore an amicable character, Her Majesty refrained from any demonstration of force. But when, in addition to the assemblage of large military forces on the frontier of Turkey, the ambassador of Russia intimated that serious consequences would ensue from the refusal of the Sultan to comply with unwarrantable demands, Her Majesty deemed it right, in conjunction with the Emperor of the French, to give an unquestionable proof of her determination to support the sovereign rights of the Sultan.

"The Russian government has maintained that the determination of the Emperor to occupy the Principalities was taken in consequence of the advance of the fleets of England and France. But the menace of invasion of the Turkish territory was conveyed in Count Nesselrode's note to Reschid Pacha, of the 19th (31st) May, and re-stated in his despatch to Baron Brunow, of the 20th May, (1st June,) which announced the determination of the Emperor of Russia to order his troops to occupy the Principalities, if the Porte did not within a week comply with the demands of Russia.

"The despatch to Her Majesty's ambassador at Constantinople authorizing him, in certain specified contingencies, to send for the British fleet, was dated the 31st of May, and the order sent direct from England to Her Majesty's admiral to proceed to the neighborhood of the Dardanelles was dated the 2d of June.

"The determination to occupy the Principalities was, therefore, taken before the orders for the advance of the combined squadron were given.

"The Sultan's Minister was informed that unless he signed within a week, and without the change of a word, the note proposed to the Porte by Prince Menschikoff, on the eve of his departure from Constantinople, the Principalities of Moldavia and Wallachia would be occupied by Russian troops. The Sultan could not accede to so insulting a demand; but when the actual occupation of the Principalities took place, the Sultan did not, as he might have done in the exercise of his undoubted right, declare war, but addressed a protest to his allies.

"Her Majesty, in conjunction with the sovereigns of Austria, France, and Prussia, has made various attempts to meet any just demands of the Emperor of Russia, without affecting the dignity and independence of the Sultan; and had it been the sole object of Russia to obtain security for the enjoyment by the Christian subjects of the Porte of their privileges and immunities, she would have found it in the offers that have been made by the Sultan. But as that security was not offered in the shape of a special and separate stipulation with Russia, it was rejected. Twice has this offer been made by the Sultan, and recommended by the Four Powers: once by a note originally prepared at Vienna, and subsequently modified by the Porte; once by the proposal of bases of negotiations agreed upon at Constantinople on the 31st of December, and approved at Vienna on the 13th of January, as offering to the two parties the means of arriving at an understanding in a becoming and honorable manner.

"It is thus manifest that a right for Russia to interfere in the ordinary relations of Turkish subjects to their sovereign, and not the happiness of Christian communities in Turkey, was the object sought for by the Russian government. To such a demand the Sultan would not submit, and his Highness, in self-defence, declared war upon Russia; but Her Majesty, nevertheless, in conjunction with her allies, has not ceased her endeavors to restore peace between the contending parties.

"The time has, however, now arrived when the advice and remonstrances of the Four Powers having proved wholly ineffectual, and the military preparations of Russia becoming daily more extended, it is but too obvious that the Emperor of Russia has entered upon a course of policy which, if unchecked, must lead to the destruction of the Ottoman Empire.

"In this conjecture, Her Majesty feels called upon by regard for an ally, the integrity and independence of whose empire have been recognised as essential to the peace of Europe, by the sympathies of her people with right against wrong, by a desire to avert from her dominions most injurious consequences, and to save Europe from the preponderance of a Power which has violated the faith of treaties, and defies the opinion of the civilized world, to take up arms, in conjunction with the Emperor of the French, for the defence of the Sultan.

"Her Majesty is persuaded that in so acting she will have the cordial support of her people; and that the pretext of zeal for the Christian religion will be used in vain to cover an aggression, undertaken in disregard of its holy precepts and of its pure and beneficent spirit.

"Her Majesty humbly trusts that her efforts may be successful, and that, by the blessing of Providence, peace may be re-established on safe and solid foundations.

"WESTMINSTER, March 28, 1854."

IV.

ADMINISTRATION OF JUSTICE.

THE Ottoman empire is governed by a code of laws called *multeka*, founded on the precepts of the Koran, the oral laws of Mohammed, his traditions, usages, and opinions, together with the sentences and decisions of the early caliphs, and the doctors of the first ages of Islamism. This code comprises a collection of laws relating to religious, civil, criminal, political, and military affairs; all equally respected as being theocratical, canonical, and immutable, though obligatory in different degrees, according to the authority which accompanies each precept. In some instances it imposes a duty of eternal obligation, as being a transcript of the divine will as revealed to the prophet: in others it invites to an imitation of the prophet in his life and conduct. And though to slight the example be blamable, it does not entail upon the delinquent the imputation or penalty of guilt; while the decisions of doctors on questions that have arisen since the death of the prophet are of still inferior authority. When a matter occurs that has not been foreseen or provided for by the early promulgators of the law, the Sultan pronounces a decision; and his authority is absolute in all matters that do not interfere with the doctrines or practical duties of religion. The code *multeka* is, however, alone considered as paramount law: the decisions or decrees of the Sultan (hatti scheriff), of which a compilation was made by Solyman the Magnificent, under the name of *canon nameh*, are considered as emanations from human authority, and, as such, are susceptible of modification, or even abolition, remaining in force only during the pleasure of the Sultan or his successors. (*Thornton*, i. 107, &c.) The *adet* or provincial customs are also allowed considerable influence.

In all the districts and towns of the empire, justice is administered by judges (*cadis*), who are of five different ranks, according to the importance of the place in which they are established, each cadi being assisted by a deputy, or *naib*. Nothing can be more simple and expeditious than the forms of proceeding in Turkish courts. Each party represents his case, unassisted by counsellors, advocates, or pleaders of any kind, and supports his statements by the production of evidence. The deposition of two competent witnesses is admitted as complete legal proof in all cases whatever.

The promptitude of Turkish justice has been often praised; but though dilatoriness be, in this respect, highly blamable, we apprehend that it is a far less evil than the other extreme. In Turkey, no ordinary legal authority can detain an untried man in prison more than three days; and in criminal cases the execution of sentences follows close upon the decision of the judge; but neither of these regulations appears to be advantageous; for, in the one case, sufficient time is not allowed to prepare either a defence or an accusation; and in the other, the immediate execution of the sentence prevents the power of appeal to a superior tribunal, and consequently takes away the only means of getting an unjust decision reversed, and, what is of more consequence, an unjust or ignorant judge exposed and degraded. In the greater number of civil cases appeals may be made from the *naib* to the *cadi*, from the latter to the *cadi-asker*, or judge of the province, and hence to the Sultan. The latter, however, is rarely practised; and is effected only by presenting a petition to his highness on his way to the mosque. Bastinado, fine, imprisonment, the galleys, and capital punishment by hanging, drowning, beheading, or strangling, are the principal means of disposing of criminals. Death is sometimes awarded for what we should consider comparatively venial crimes, as, for instance, unfair dealing on the part of tradesmen; though a butcher or baker convicted of short weight is more frequently nailed by the ear to the door of his shop.

Speaking generally, the administration of justice is in the most disgraceful state in Turkey. According to law, all the judgments of the pachas and of their deputies should be submitted to the cadi, and can only be legally carried into effect when approved by the latter. But, in practice, this salutary regulation is generally disregarded, and in most cases the sentences of the pacha are executed whether they be approved by the cadi or not. (*Boué*, iii. 351.) But the grand vice of Turkish justice consists in the venality of the judges and the toleration of perjury. "The monarch's despotism is not the greatest evil in Turkey: his subjects would, perhaps, bear that without much murmuring or great distress. The radical destruction of all security lies in the iniquitous administration of their laws, which are an impending sword in the hand of corruption, ever ready to cut off their lives and properties." (*Porter*, ii. 1.) Mr. Thornton seems to think that Turks have rarely to complain of injustice, and that, speaking generally, the decisions of the judges, in cases where both parties are Mussulmans, are fair and impartial. We are assured, however, by those well acquainted with the fact, that this statement must be received with great modification, and that a rich or powerful Turk has, in most instances, little or no difficulty in obtaining a decision in his favor, however unjust his cause; and that as respects Christians and Jews, they have no chance in a litigation with a Turk, unless they succeed beforehand in securing the good offices of the judge. It is a principle of Turkish law that written testimony is of no avail when opposed to living witnesses; and hence every precaution should be taken to render the latter trustworthy. But, instead of this, the most detestable perjurers enjoy an all but total impunity, and carry on a lucrative as well as an infamous profession. False swearing is punished by leading the culprit through the streets seated on an ass, with his face turned to the animal's tail; and even this punishment, trifling as it is when imposed on such wretches, is rarely enforced. Magistrates are compelled to decide according to the evidence of notorious perjurers, unless they detect their falsehood at the moment. The subjects of foreign powers residing in Turkey are allowed, in virtue of treaties to that effect, to support their claims by written evidence. (*Thornton*, i. 196, &c.)

M. Boué, whose remarks on the administration of justice are as superficial as can well be imagined, is good enough to inform his readers that *si on ne pouvait pas citer de faux témoins, des témoins subornés à prix d'argent, et même des juges qui se laissent gagner, la justice Turque mériterait tout aussi bien ce nom que la nôtre!* (iii. 355.) True, and on the same principle we might say that if A. were not a thief, he would be as honest as B.

There is a considerable discrepancy in the accounts of the state of the police in Turkey, though most recent travellers say that it is extremely defective. No doubt, however, considering the abuses inherent in every department of the administration, it is superior to what might have been expected. This is mainly ascribable to the regulation which makes every district of the country responsible for all the murders, robberies, and other crimes of violence committed within its bounds; and which consequently makes their repression the business of all the more respectable inhabitants.

Owing to the jealousy of the Turks of the invasion of their privacy, no writ of search can at any time be executed in the interior of the house of a Turk but in the presence of the Iman, nor in that of a Christian except accompanied by a priest; nor of a Jew, unless a rabbi be present. The rooms occupied by the women, which are never entered, frequently shelter criminals.—*From M'Culloch's Geog. Dic.*

THE END.

www.ingramcontent.com/pod-product-compliance
Lightning Source LLC
LaVergne TN
LVHW011205110826
845150LV00006B/1326
* 9 7 8 1 4 2 5 5 1 8 9 7 4 *